RIGHTANGLE
PUBLISHING

Brindleyplace: a model for urban regeneration

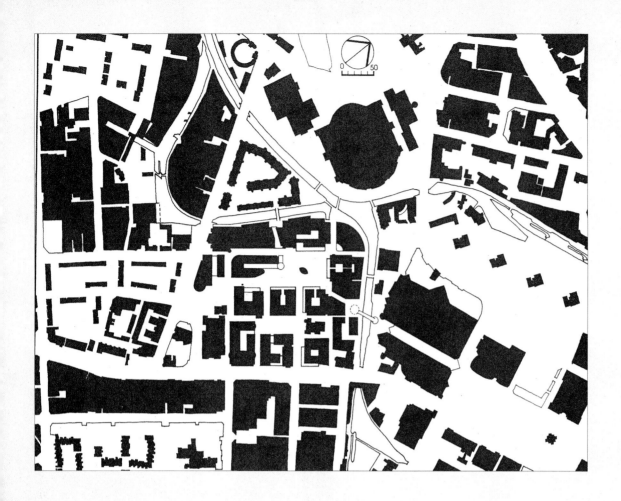

First published in the UK by:
Right Angle Publishing Ltd,
161 Rosebery Avenue,
London EC1R 4QX.

Edited and designed by
Ian Latham and Mark Swenarton.

Printed in the UK.

British Library Cataloguing in Publication
Data. A catalogue record for this book
is available from the British Library.

ISBN 0 9532848 1 6

RIGHTANGLE
PUBLISHING

Brindleyplace: a model for urban regeneration

edited by Ian Latham and Mark Swenarton

Introduction

Ian Latham and Mark Swenarton

In the first cities which evolved around six thousand years ago – the 'cradles of civilisation' – were laid the roots of the social and political structures that characterise the modern world. Over the centuries, economies of urban scale spawned remarkable cultural and scientific achievements, but they also brought the inequality, deprivation and conflict which now seem all too apparent in the contemporary urban condition.

The contemporary malaise in our cities takes many forms. Businesses relocate from city centres to peripheral business parks where rents, rates and labour costs are low. Retailers move from the high street to out-of-town sites. Families abandon the inner city for the suburbs in search of fresh air, good schools and safety from traffic and crime. Deterioration and decline set in as the mobile affluent move out and those left behind suffer the multiple deprivations of unemployment, low income, poor housing and substandard health and leisure facilities.

How then are our cities to be made attractive again to employers and employees, residents and consumers? The story of Brindleyplace – the reversal in fortunes of a major site in inner-city Birmingham – could well hold the answer.

Not so long ago Birmingham was held, only part in jest, as the greatest disaster of modern urban planning. Lacking the robust qualities of Liverpool or Manchester, the city centre was regulated for the convenience of traffic and what character it possessed was choked by the notorious inner ring road – even the shopping centre was in a 'Bull Ring'. But all that has changed. Nowadays it is possible to walk from New Street Station along pedestrianised streets and through a series of public spaces to the International Convention Centre. From here the route continues over the canal to Brindleyplace, where a new landscaped square forms the heart of the UK's largest inner-city mixed-use development. With its dense mix of office buildings, housing, shops, restaurants and cafes, and even an art gallery and theatre, Brindleyplace has been hailed as a model for the city of the future.

The Brindleyplace site is a classic by-product of the industrial revolution. Adjoining Broad Street, the historic 'high road' linking the working city centre to the affluent residential outpost of Edgbaston, the site boundaries were effectively defined in 1772 with the cutting of the Birmingham and Brindley Loop canals. For nearly two centuries it was a bustling mass of wharves, canal boats and workshops, as Birmingham's metal-bashers produced the pots, pans and bedsteads that were exported around the world. But in the second half of the twentieth century Birmingham's metal trades succumbed to the forces of international competition and the factories and wharves closed down.

Thanks to the far-sighted policies of the city council and the vision of the developer Argent (led by Michael and Peter Freeman and Roger Madelin), this industrial wasteland has been transformed into a showpiece development of public squares and buildings. But rather than characteristic post-war 'zoned planning' with its dedicated sectors – housing, work, retail, leisure etc – the model for Brindleyplace is the traditional European city where living, working and recreation all take place in close proximity. The plan comprises a network of streets and public spaces lined by arcaded buildings, harmonious in materials and massing. Offices, some with cafes and restaurants at ground level (and some with apartments above), are placed alongside cultural and leisure facilities and the housing is only the width of a canal bridge from the workplace.

Mixed-use developments such as this are widely promoted as a way of breathing life back into our cities. In the age of polluting heavy industries, planners forced factories and housing into separate zones. But in the post-industrial world, the rationale for separating work and home no longer exists. On the contrary, to do so positively encourages the use of private cars, with their well-documented damage to the planet. For ecological reasons if no other, mixed use is integral to the sustainable city.

Brindleyplace echoes the traditional European city not just in the variety of uses but also in the priority given to the public realm. The concern is as much with the quality of spaces between buildings as with the buildings themselves. The designers and developers have recognised that what makes the historic city so rich is the array of public spaces that it provides. History suggests too that well-defined urban spaces tend to outlast their surrounding buildings, which come and go over

Brindleyplace as a cleared site, looking towards the city centre; the masterplan model; and the development in 1999.

time, contributing significantly to urban variety.

At the heart of Brindleyplace is a landscaped square (completed in advance of the buildings) with fountains, cafe and grass terraces and surrounded by street-level arcades to the buildings. In front of the Ikon Gallery a second square has been formed, calmer in detail but enlivened by restaurants and cafes. Streets have been designed to indicate priority for pedestrians while still accommodating vehicles. As well as being commercially difficult, the segregation of traffic would have been inconsistent with the mixed-use approach. Both in their alignment and levels, new streets have been carefully positioned to integrate with the pattern of the adjacent streets, establishing continuity with the grain of the city and 'blurring' the boundaries of Brindleyplace.

This holistic approach to the streetscape is familiar in some out-of-town business parks, such as Stockley Park near London's Heathrow airport, but all too rare in the inner city. At Brindleyplace however it was adopted for sound commercial reasons – to establish and maintain the desirability of the address for potential office tenants – and there is no reason why the approach should not work elsewhere. In effect a way has to be found for the long-term interest of building owners to be translated, if necessary through the mechanisms of local government, into the effective design and management of the surrounding public realm.

At Brindleyplace the commitment to design quality and richness was integral to the whole development, from masterplanning through to the public spaces and buildings. The scheme avoids the deadening effect of having a single hand designing all the buildings, while also preventing the architectural zoo that could result from using a variety of architects, if each of their buildings tried to out-do its neighbours. Masterplanning guidelines were drawn up covering strategic matters such as massing and the selection of materials; most buildings share a tripartite elevational treatment with a base (street-level arcade), middle (repetitive office floor plates) and top (roof-level plant).

The design of the various office buildings was entrusted to half-a-dozen different architectural practices, all of them with an established reputation for design quality and – equally important – all of them willing to work alongside one another within an evolving masterplan. No attempt was made to dictate stylistic uniformity – indeed the chosen architects represent a diverse range of interests, from the new classicism of Porphyrios Associates to the cool modernity of Stanton Williams. The bringing together, by careful selection, of some of the best UK architects to work in a neighbourly fashion is in itself no small achievement.

The merits of this approach can now be appreciated on site. While observing the requirements of the masterplan and respecting their neighbours, the buildings all have their own character. Where Number Five has curved brick walls with punched windows, the cafe is dramatically cased in glass, while the Ikon Gallery has been creatively formed out of a red-brick Victorian school building. As in a 'real' city, where richness and variety are the norm, no one will like every building at Brindleyplace but neither will any one person dislike them all.

But what made Brindleyplace possible? Here again the development offers important lessons. The scheme would never have happened without the planning and land acquisition policies pursued by Birmingham city council in the 1980s. What eventually became the Brindleyplace site was acquired over a number of years (by open and compulsory purchase) as part of the scheme for the International Convention Centre (including Symphony Hall) and associated leisure facilities.

But a further unforeseen factor was involved in the genesis of Brindleyplace – a massive fall in the market value of the site. With the extraordinary turbulence that hit the UK property markets in the late 80s and early 90s, land that had been sold in 1988 for about one million pounds per acre (more than two million pounds per hectare) changed hands five years later for less than a fifth of that amount. The loser in this was the developer Rosehaugh, which went into liquidation and from whose receivers Argent acquired the site. Had Argent had to pay anything like the previous value, it could not have been so generous in the allocation of (and expenditure on) public space and community facilities. Without the hidden subsidy delivered by the collapse of the property market, Brindleyplace would have been very different.

But Brindleyplace is not just about planning

policies and architectural designs; it is also the built reality of bricks and mortar. Here too the development has broader implications both for urban regeneration and for the procurement of buildings. Peculiar to the UK construction industry is the chain of contracts which connects the various parties – client, consultants, main contractor, sub-contractors, suppliers – binding them to the performance of specific tasks but giving them no interest in the overall delivery of the product. Delays, cost over-runs and low standards are seen as part-and-parcel of a process in which a primary concern of those involved is to protect themselves from litigation.

Little wonder then that major clients – not least the government – have sought to replace this adversarial system with a method focused on product delivery. The 1998 report by Sir John Egan, former chairman of Jaguar, called for construction to adopt the techniques of supply management used in the automotive industry. In particular Egan called for the 'partnering' of the supply chain, so that, instead of going out to competitive tender, the procurer develops long-term relationships with the key suppliers. This programme is being actively pursued by the Department of the Environment, Transport and the Regions (DETR) with a view to cutting costs, eliminating delays and improving quality in the UK construction industry.

Long before it became fashionable in government and industry circles, Argent had adopted partnering as the procurement method for Brindleyplace and established the methods for carrying it out. The company 'partners' with contractors (as well as sub-contractors) on a long-term basis, ensuring value-for-money not by the usual route of competitive tendering but by 'benchmarking', measuring costs against those of similar buildings elsewhere. With Argent now applauded by the DETR, Brindleyplace stands as one of the most important demonstrations to date of partnering in construction.

With this book the development of Brindleyplace is fully documented for the first time. In Chapter One, Professor David Dunster sets the context by highlighting some major themes in urban design since the beginning of the twentieth century. In Chapter Two, Joe Holyoak traces the history of the Brindleyplace site over the same period, charting Birmingham's plans for regenerating the city centre and taking the story up to the purchase of the site by Argent in 1993. The narrative then passes to those directly involved in the development. In Chapter Three, John Chatwin, who has worked on Brindleyplace throughout, explains the evolution of the masterplan. In Chapter Four, Roger Madelin of Argent reveals how the partnership with architects, contractors, Birmingham city and tenants has helped make Brindleyplace a real piece of city. In Chapter Five, Argent's David Partridge focuses on the choice of architects and the design and development of the individual buildings and squares. Finally in Chapter Six, Professor Patsy Healey assesses the wider significance of Brindleyplace for the policies and practices of urban regeneration.

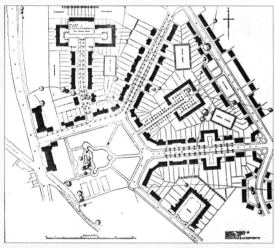

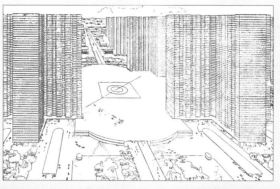

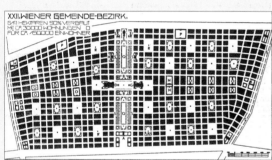

XXII. WIENER GEMEINDE-BEZIRK.

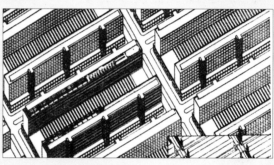

Chapter one: A century of urban design

David Dunster

As this century closes, the future of cities has returned to a place on the political stage. Around a hundred years ago the issue of how to make cities liveable addressed the problem of horse-drawn traffic and the products of the equine urban population, in much the same way as we now worry about pollution from mechanical transport. Between 1900 and 1914 the solutions offered were either to leave the city for the idyll of the suburb, midway between the Great Wens and an agricultural countryside; or to beautify that which was ugly within the city, bring order to chaos and plan the future.

In Europe the garden city movement unwittingly played into the hands of the mass housebuilding industry, which ate up the land released by agricultural decline to produce today's suburban 'delights'. In America the city beautiful movement failed to build on the consensus established between business and government and fell victim to the ever-growing demands of the automotive manufacturers for roads for their vehicles. Whatever was achieved in each case in the first half of this century merely scratched the surface of urban development – and certainly had less effect than the bombing campaigns of the second world war and later international programmes for building highways. It was as if the cities which persisted from earlier times were now irrelevant.

That blindness to the qualities of many centuries of urban growth received enormous encouragement from the manifestos of the architectural modern movement. For the modernists, the existing cities in which they worked, lived, met their clients, and supported the avant-garde were inconsequential, to be rebuilt in images of the future which, like Le Corbusier's and Ludwig Hilberseimer's various plans of the 20s, demolished vast areas as if the emerging complexity of property ownership could

be swept aside by a benign despot. In images of chilling audacity, the most forward-thinking architects provided a new formal discourse. Occasionally landowners toyed with the novel. In the 30s the promoters of projects such as Villeurbanne near Lyon and the Rockefeller Centre in New York adopted the idea of renewal deriving from those manifestos but clad the forms in art deco style.

By 1950, what a modern city might look like was still a mystery. European urban rebuilding first dealt with housing, which became the major theme of planning. The post-war new towns constructed in Britain adopted ideas of community size based on educational provision. Invariably these projects contained little of a truly urban scale, working over themes already established by Unwin and the garden city movement. In contrast the new towns constructed around Paris tried to ape metropolitan densities but again concentrated upon housing provision. Analysis of cities was however beginning to change blindness into focus.

Since the enlightenment, cities had been diagnosed as if they were diseased. The earliest metropolitan authorities were established, in London and in New York for example, to regulate the supply of potable water and to drain away waste products. During the nineteenth century diseases carried by water were gradually brought under control. Cities were explained as if they were human bodies, with parks as lungs, roads and streets as arteries and the heart always some metaphysical centre (curiously universities were never considered to be the brains). The medical analogy scored heavily over any more formal analysis of cities. For example the theories of the late nineteenth-century Viennese architect Camillo Sitte took the urban patterns of Italy as a model for the development of Vienna, a rearguard argument conducted largely after the

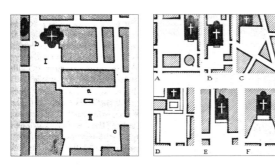

Maurice Leroux, Avenue de l'Hôtel de Ville, Villeurbanne (1931-34); Reinhard & Hofmeister, Corbett Harrison & Macmurray, Raymond Hood, Godley & Fouilhoux, Rockefeller Centre, New York (1931-40); Raymond Hood, A City of Towers (1927).

transformation of Vienna's military glacis into the Ringstrasse. But Sitte's dream of bringing Italian urban forms to the Habsburg empire remained largely unrealised. Similarly, the city beautiful movement in America proposed urban development explicitly copied from Haussmann's transformation of Paris. But again the block forms that resulted in the evocative perspectives in the Plan of Chicago lost out to the pervasive skyscraper. A formal analysis of city structure would have to wait until the 1960s.

What was the conception of the city in the postwar period? Any answer would certainly have to refer to the strength of the interest groups who could make their voices heard. While a new profession of planners emerged, what called them into play was the political decision to regulate growth and change in cities by means of planning legislation. Local government was required to draw up plans which structured future potential. The categories used – density, land use, transport infrastructure and existing ownership rights – mirrored a shift away from the idea of the city as a body. Now it was viewed as a machine, subject to scientific examination via numerical sociology. Cities were conceived as 'networks' in which 'nodes' grew where 'flows' intersected. Insofar as prediction was possible, it was based on harnessing the demands of a supply-based economy – except within the socialist East where a demand economy still allowed the last examples of planning by fiat. But these republics turned against modernism as a bourgeois weakness and espoused instead a neoclassicism that was said to be understood by the people. Formal analysis here was therefore stylistic.

In the 60s in the West the authority of planning came under question on a variety of fronts. Firstly, the new building programmes failed to produce

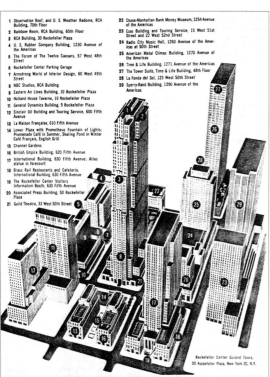

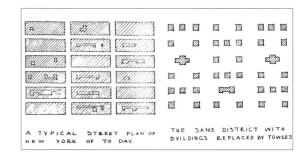

A TYPICAL STREET PLAN OF NEW YORK OF TO DAY.   THE SAME DISTRICT WITH BUILDINGS REPLACED BY TOWERS

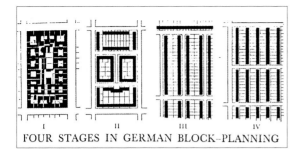

FOUR STAGES IN GERMAN BLOCK-PLANNING

the benefits that the modernist manifestos had claimed, leading to a powerful disaffection for the architectural style employed. Secondly, cities increasingly abandoned for suburbs became economically and spatially attractive to marginal interests – artists in New York's SoHo seeking large workspaces or the younger professional middle-class seeking housing near their work in London, Paris and West Berlin. Thirdly, nostalgia for places now visitable in an age of increasing mass transport suggested that the functionalist pseudo-scientific approach to planning might not be enough to guarantee a desirable future.

By the 80s architects had rediscovered the work of Sitte, with his formal analysis of Italian squares; exhumed the eighteenth-century plan of Rome drawn by Nolli, in which indoor and outdoor public space was shown alike as white while private space was shown as black; and began to revisit arguments dating from nineteenth-century France about building typology. An analytical framework for dealing with cities as they existed developed under the all-embracing rubric of context. The change, from the attitudes enshrined in planning laws designed to permit the reconstruction of devastated cities to the context-driven attitudes of architectural thinking begun in the 60s, has still not entirely worked through to the statutory instruments of planning. But the brashness of the modern movement's rejection of history and hence of the city formed in history was rewritten.

This changed awareness required a new terminology. Crucial was the recognition of the fundamental importance of the 'urban block'. This can be seen at its clearest in cities such as Barcelona and Madrid, where construction has proceeded along the pattern laid out by road grids while development is restricted in terms of height but invariably

Catherine Bauer, Four Stages in German Block Planning, from Modern Housing (1934); Bruno Taut, Martin Wagner et al, Großsiedlung Britz, Berlin (1925-31); Shadrach Woods, masterplan for new town of Toulouse-Le-Mirail (1960); Frederick Gibberd, Harlow New Town, central district (1948); Alexanderplatz reconstruction, East Berlin (1969)

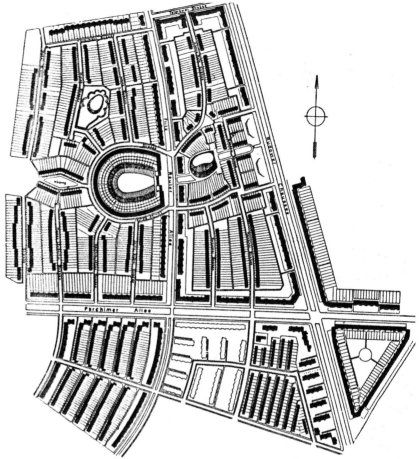

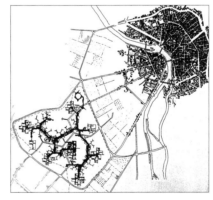

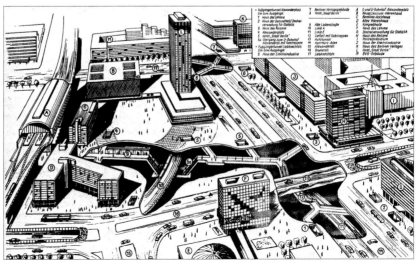

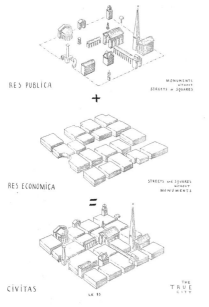

RES PUBLICA

MONUMENTS
WITHOUT
STREETS OR SQUARES

+

RES ECONOMICA

STREETS AND SQUARES
WITHOUT
MONUMENTS

=

CIVITAS

LK 83

THE
TRUE
CITY

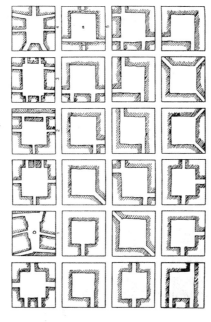

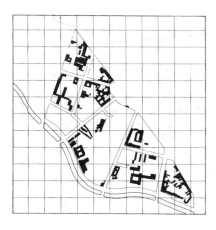

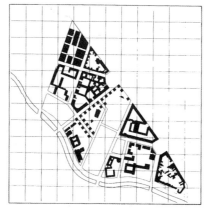

mixed in use. The urban block in this regard is not to be confused here simply with urban patterns produced by road layouts; the blocks are deep and the building facades form a continuous street front on all four sides. The difference between the 'street' and the 'avenue' provided by the New York grid does not obtain and the block therefore faces equally in all directions – any difference between front and back is contained within it.

These urban blocks consist of types of building which are defined not by function but by form. This means for example that the arcade must be considered an urban form whereas a school cannot. An urban type is defined by its function within the city plan, not by the function which it houses. In the UK context, the closest we seem to approach this meaning is in describing single buildings which have many uses – the multi-use building to use the argot of architects.

One final term concerns the idea of what belongs to the public, as opposed to what belongs to the individual. Public space, and its imputed demise, is perhaps the most vexed term to define. Does it mean for example spaces in which the ideal citizenry can gather to arrive at decisions concerning their future and that of their polis? Does it mean space where individuals can walk freely, whether they are pensioners or prostitutes? The urban block, type, and public space are all terms which occur in no modernist manifestos but which Brindleyplace employs to define its objectives.

Birmingham's city centre is shaped somewhat like a tadpole, with the commercial and retail district forming the body and Broad Street the tail. Now connecting the two is Brindleyplace, which extends the city centre with a masterplan based more on European than local precedent. While there still seem some remnants of functional expression in the

Rob Krier, medium-scale urban space, from Stadtraum (1975); Leon Krier, the True City (1983); Rob Krier, morphological series of urban spaces, from Stadtraum (1975); OM Ungers, plan for Friedrichstadt, Berlin (1981), existing (left) and proposed; Aldo Rossi, Analagous City (1976).

architecture, the central building by Demetri Porphyrios could house any of a variety of uses. In urban terms he has read the purpose of this block correctly – it is the centrepiece of the first phase which holds the other buildings together. If the masterplan has a weakness, it is surely the positioning (and sadly the design) of the National Sealife Centre, which is formally alien to the urban plan; what does a stingray have to do with a city? By contrast the buildings that define the main square are a quiet, elegant exercise in polite and cosmopolitan urbanism – precisely the architecture which should derive from an analysis of urban block forms, types and public spaces.

Each of the buildings is located within a spatial array which makes substantial demands on the architects. The buildings have to face the square, in order for it to be a substantial public space; but they must also face Birmingham with their backs. This problem is not new in the long-term history of cities, but seems novel to some of the architects. Buildings are horizontally linked with fairly gracious arcades around the square but this device (well used in Bologna, Padua, Milan and Paris) does not extend to the rest of the surrounding urban fabric, where it would have challenged the reluctance of British cities to provide shelter within new developments. Nevertheless the scheme, the UK's largest inner-city development since London's Broadgate in the late 80s, sounds a trumpet for the urban theories which architects and historians have developed over the last 30 years. This is not utopia: but it is a very civilised holding action.

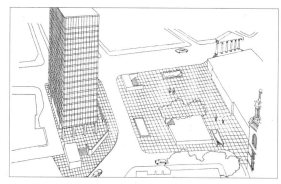

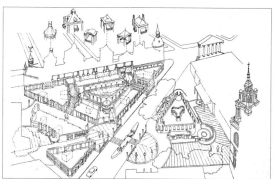

Terry Farrell, project for Mansion House and Poultry, City of London (1984-5), showing the 'official' Mies van der Rohe 1967 scheme (top) and Farrell's counter-proposal (right); Terry Farrell, Brindleyplace masterplan (1991) showing the site in 1834, 1918, 1990 and as proposed.

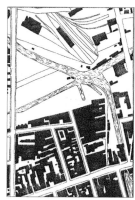

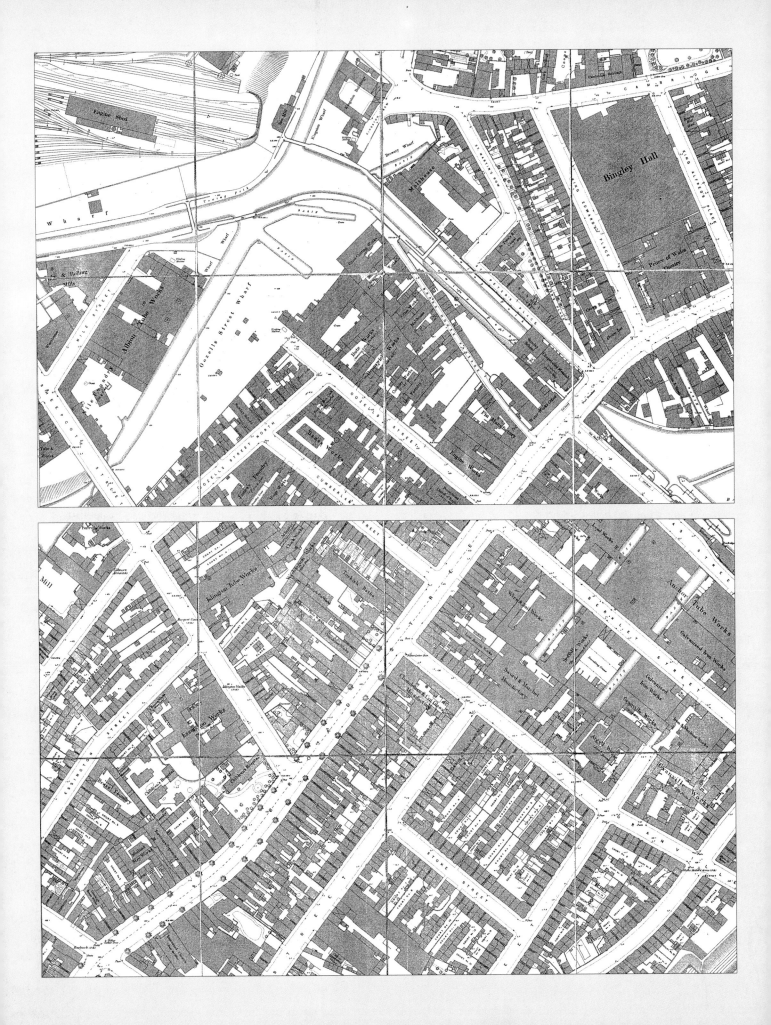

Chapter two: City edge – before Brindleyplace

Joe Holyoak

The redevelopment of the western edge of Birmingham's city centre, where Brindleyplace now stands, has been an objective for much of the twentieth century. Successive schemes, including Brindleyplace, progressed unpredictably in a snakes-and-ladders way that, if nothing else, shows that making plans and implementing them are quite different things.

The commercial and retail centre of Birmingham was hemmed in by the industry that arrived with the canals in the late-eighteenth century; as the city prospered and expanded over the next 100 years, its centre seemed increasingly inadequate. The west side was long seen as special. Firstly, because the nineteenth century's honorific civic grouping of town hall, Council House, museum and art gallery plus the library was on the western edge of the city centre, grouped around Victoria Square and Chamberlain Place. Secondly, because only three-quarters of a mile from Chamberlain Place, at the other end of the radial route of Broad Street, was the high-status area of Edgbaston. While lying outside the city centre proper, up until the 1950s Broad Street formed a strip of prestigious shopping, cutting through the industrial hinterland which divided the city centre from Edgbaston.

In 1930 a competition was announced for a new civic centre to be built on Broad Street. The site was immediately beyond the point where later the inner ring road would run around the city centre. The resultant scheme by Cecil Howitt was an imposing beaux-arts design with five neoclassical buildings arranged around a huge square. But at the outbreak of war in 1939, only half of one building (now called Baskerville House) had been constructed and after the war the scheme was abandoned.

In the 50s it was decided that a new civic centre should be created inside the line of the inner ring road, whose design was then being finalised. This proved to be a second uncompleted scheme. The new central library and school of music (by John Madin Design Group) were built but the rest was abandoned in a financial crisis of the 70s. Together with the inner ring road (named the Queensway), the half-built site created a huge gash between the city centre and the Broad Street area.

The catastrophic decline in the city's manufacturing economy in the 70s led the city council to look for a new economic base for the city. One of the elements of this was to be the construction of the International Convention Centre, the biggest conference venue in the UK. Eventually the site for this was chosen in Broad Street, on part of the 1930 civic centre site. The Broad Street Redevelopment Area was designated, running west from the Queensway with, beyond the ICC site, a large zone of canalside industry and derelict land – the area that was to become Brindleyplace. In the 1983 ICC feasibility study, this zone was designated mainly for entertainment and leisure facilities to support the ICC, with some office development and car parking including 1600 car spaces for the ICC.

The ICC was to be funded by public money, mostly from the European Community; the ancillary area of 10 hectares on the other side of the canal was to be developed by the private sector. The city council carried out the necessary land assembly and in 1987 drew up a development brief, as the basis for bids by developers. The development was to provide complementary facilities for visitors to the ICC, centred on a 'festival marketplace' canalside scheme. This idea derived from the visit that the planning committee and officers had made to the USA in 1984 to investigate American convention centres, where they had been greatly impressed by the James Rouse developments of Baltimore Harbour and Boston's Faneuil Hall Marketplace. These waterside tourist magnets formed the model for the 1987 development brief.

As well as the 'heritage attraction' and car parking (now increased to 2,800 cars and 30 coaches), the other mandatory component of the development was the National Indoor Arena. The indoor arena (originally specifically for athletics, but later to become multi-purpose) had been regarded by the city council as a priority for some time; various sites had been proposed before the Broad Street Redevelopment Area was chosen and the city architect, William Reed, had designed a building for this site before it was decided to hand the project over to the private sector. The city council offered up to £19m for the development cost. As well as the indoor arena, the development brief specified a range of other possible components, mostly leisure or retail. At the very bottom of the list, it stated that 'additionally, residential or office accommodation will be acceptable, as part of a larger mixed-use scheme'. How priorities were to change! The site was cleared of its factories and warehouses, leaving the 1964 Crescent Theatre (in the centre) and the empty and boarded-up grade 2 listed Oozells Street School, dating from 1877. The brief specified that the indoor arena was to be completed by spring 1990 and the rest of the development by 1991. The reality was to turn out very differently.

At this stage a fundamental change occurred in Birmingham's approach to planning. Ever since Joseph Chamberlain's mayoralty in the 1870s, Birmingham had been known for its ambitious but pragmatic approach to urban planning and development. Birmingham's developments were huge in scale, ambitious in conception and skilfully managed – but lacking in quality. Birmingham was a prosaic, 'can-do' city; a place which worked but not one from which you expected to take any pleasure.

Particularly in the doldrums of the mid-80s, city planning was driven by the imperatives of development, with a single council department combining the disciplines of town planning and economic development. In the city's drive to attract new investment, developers could set the agenda for planning. This was vividly illustrated in 1987 with the scheme for redeveloping the Bull Ring Centre, the notorious 60s planning disaster that occupied a huge site in the city centre. The city's planners had no urban design brief prepared for the site and, when the new owners submitted a redevelopment scheme, it was received enthusiastically by the planning committee, despite threatening to repeat the mistakes of the 60s all over again. A £200m investment was not to be discouraged.

But in March 1988 an event took place that was to

The 'triangle site' in 1989, shortly before demolition to make way for housing, and (below) the Brindleyplace site as it was c1970.

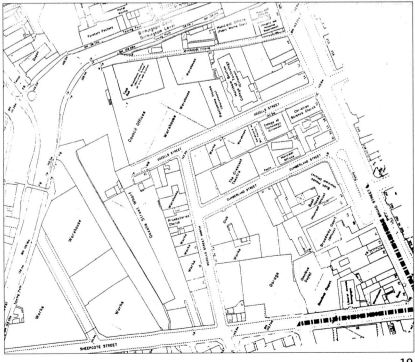

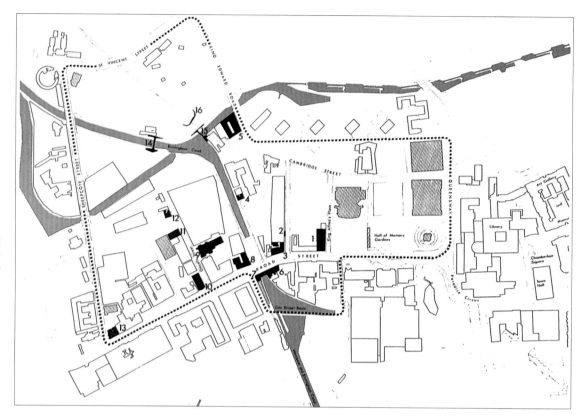

Listed buildings in the Broad Street Redevelopment Area, from the 1985 Townscape Study prepared by the Convention Centre Partnership, a collaboration between Percy Thomas Partnership and Renton Howard Wood Levin Partnership. The Brindleyplace site is on the left. 1 Bingley Buildings; 2 Men's urinals, King Edward's Place; 3 The Crown public house; 4 Brewmaster's House; 5 Nos 79-80 Cambridge Street; 6 Nos 266a and 267-271 Broad Street; 7 No 266 Broad Street; 8 The Brass House; 9 Oozells Street School (now the Ikon Gallery); 10 Christian Science Church; 11 Suffolk Works; 12 Former Eagle Inn; 13 Barclay's Bank; 14 Roving Bridge; 15 Roving Bridge; 16 Ladywood West Railway Tunnel Portal.

change the city's thinking: an intensive weekend workshop on the planning of the city centre. Later known as the Highbury Initiative, it brought together urban experts from places such as Rotterdam, Los Angeles and Tokyo as well as leading British figures (including Will Alsop, Judy Hillman, David Lock, Peter Rice and Terry Farrell) who offered new perspectives on city planning. Two key commissions followed directly: one of the Highbury participants, Don Hilderbrandt of Maryland-based consultants LDR, was commissioned to undertake a pedestrianisation plan for the city; and the UK urban design practice Tibbalds Colbourne was commissioned to undertake the Birmingham Urban Design Study (BUDS). Those managing the shaping of the city centre drew from the Highbury Initiative a realisation that quality was important; that it did not happen by accident; and that it would be produced only within a strategic framework purposefully drawn up to that end. Before Highbury, urban design was a rather foreign concept in Birmingham. After Highbury, the importance of having an urban design vision which could facilitate the right kind of new development was understood. This was the new climate in which the discussions about the development of Brindleyplace began to take place.

The 1987 invitation to developers for the festival marketplace scheme brought in 21 expressions of interest. This was reduced to a long list of eight, from which six were invited to make a financial bid. One of the six was Merlin, in association with James Rouse, the American developer of Baltimore Harbour. Their proposal focused on the festival market but the indoor arena component was not very convincing. Also in the six was a consortium of Shearwater and Laing. Shearwater was the retail arm of the prominent 80s developer Rosehaugh while Laing was a leading contractor who had a strong indoor arena scheme designed by American architects HOK. In the light of this Merlin decided to join forces with Shearwater and Laing to make a stronger combined bid.

By February 1988, the competing developers had been reduced to two, Merlin Shearwater Laing and Ladbroke City & County, neither of whose schemes contained any residential use. The view of the planning officials was that although Ladbroke was offering a higher sum, its arena was expensive and represented poorer value for money. Hitherto the main political parties on the council had taken a bipartisan approach to the development; for instance, the Broad Street Redevelopment Area had been designated under the Conservatives but when Labour took control in 1984 the development planning had continued without a pause. But this time the councillors divided on party lines with the

Merlin Shearwater Laing's winning 1988 proposal located the National Indoor Arena on the triangle site (top) and a Festival Marketplace (bottom) on the eventual Brindleyplace site. The architects were Percy Thomas Partnership (masterplan), Fitch Benoy (festival retailing) and HOK (National Indoor Arena).

Conservatives supporting Ladbroke and the ruling Labour group voting for Merlin Shearwater Laing.

Merlin Shearwater Laing paid £23.3m for the 25 acre (10 hectare) site and proceeded to build the indoor arena; this rather graceless block opened in October 1991. It was located on the part of the site north of the canal, spanning the Intercity railway line. This was inherently expensive, but it had the advantage of placing the indoor arena away from the rest of the development, on the least attractive (and least accessible) part of the site. With its completion, Laing's involvement in the scheme was finished and Shearwater and Merlin formed a new company, Brindleyplace plc, to carry out the rest of the development.

Shearwater brought in Alan Chatham, who was working for its parent company Rosehaugh, to act as the new company's project director. Chatham's dedication to the Brindleyplace project was to prove crucial in the difficult years ahead. As architects, Brindleyplace plc appointed the Percy Thomas Partnership, co-architects with RHWL of the International Convention Centre then taking shape on the other side of the canal.

Shearwater Merlin was committed to the festival market concept. Its architects' early schemes showed this element contained in a mall building, almost as large as the ICC, on the canal bank. This

It's go for big Broad St plan

By DAVID BELL

A final £280 million deal to convert run-down Broad Street into the international showpiece of Birmingham has been sealed by city officials after months of negotiations.

Included in the package signed with the Merlin, Shearwater, Laing consortium is an agreement to build a £51 million national indoor sports centre — a project on which construction work started months ago.

And acres of derelict land centred on the four canals surrounding the site are to be turned into a major tourist attraction with the development of a national aquarium, heritage exhibition, leisure facilities, cinemas and an hotel.

Named Brindleyplace after James Brindley, the engineer responsible for three of the canals, the Festival Market will also include a huge shopping complex and 600,000 sq ft of offices.

Contracts for the scheme should have been signed in March, but city councillors held off until MSL fulfilled all the promises of attractions it made to win a competition to be selected.

But Merlin's development director, Mr Keith Hainsworth, said that the agreement did not include a multi-million-pound monorail system looping the city centre which was in the consortium's submission.

Von Roll, the Swiss company behind the monorail, is providing one at the Merry Hill shopping complex at Brierley Hill and is still negotiating with Birmingham.

Coun Mrs Pat Sever, chairman of the International Convention Centre committee, said: "This is one of the most exciting regeneration schemes ever seen in this country."

The 8,000-seat national indoor arena will have a six-lane, 200-metre athletic track which can be converted into an ice hockey rink.

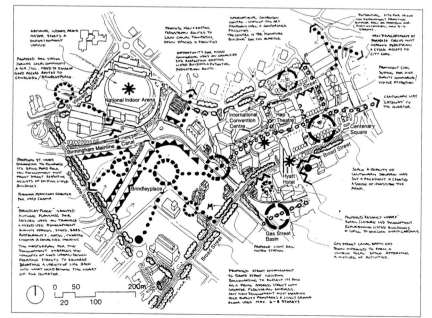

was never to be built, although it lingered on in plans for a long time. There was also a multiplex cinema, an aquarium, hotel and offices. But in hindsight the festival marketplace idea looks inherently flawed. Shearwater Merlin secured the site at the height of the property market boom. Merlin planned to transfer profits from its development in Darling Harbour, Australia, and invest them in Brindleyplace but it became involved in litigation on the Australian scheme and in mid-1989 it withdrew from the Brindleyplace deal.

The years from 1989 to 1991 saw the Brindleyplace development going nowhere, with the project team operating from a single-storey hut on Broad Street. Apart from the indoor arena, which was under construction, the other 17 acres (seven hectares) of the site remained empty and derelict, with Brindleyplace plc's parent company, Shearwater, unwilling or unable to risk investment at a time when its own financial stability was beginning to look uncertain.

For a long period, the developer met at fortnightly intervals with Geoff Wright, the planning officer in charge of the council's city centre team, to discuss the way ahead – discussions that laid the foundations for the eventual success of Brindleyplace. They were influenced, among other things, by Rosehaugh Stanhope's Broadgate and the Birmingham Urban Design Study (BUDS). In the Broadgate development on the eastern edge of the City of London, Rosehaugh Stanhope had succeeded in selling a lot of offices in a location that was 'off-traditional pitch' but well served by public transport; placemaking and new squares were seen as critical to its success. BUDS, which was adopted as policy by the city council in March 1990, also emphasised the importance of placemaking, of the 'necklace of places' and unhindered pedestrian movement. Wright was at this time also working on the Hilderbrandt pedestrianisation proposals, which were later to be one of the starting points for Terry Farrell Partnership's masterplan for Brindleyplace.

The internal festival market idea was rejected and replaced with a more varied and permeable arrangement of buildings. The retail architect Fitch Benoy was brought in to design a concentration of bars and restaurants (the Water's Edge) on the canalside opposite the ICC. But Shearwater was in

financial difficulties; in 1990 it went into liquidation and the ownership of both Brindleyplace plc and the site reverted to Rosehaugh and its chairman Godfrey Bradman. It was a further downhill lurch in the calamitous decline of the project – there would be another yet to come. But with Bradman's enforced involvement came some key decisions which would shape the project for good.

Rosehaugh decided a change of direction was needed and brought in the Terry Farrell Partnership to make a new masterplan. Under Chatham's direction, the proportion of offices in the scheme had increased and this continued. Bradman was not interested in retail and this was to disappear from the plan altogether. The first draft of the masterplan appeared in February 1991, based on a joint briefing by the city and developer. At this stage it contained no housing (Bradman was not keen on this either) while a remnant of the mall building still survived on the canalside.

Despite the embarrassing delays – the Queen was due to open the ICC in June, so the developer turfed the empty canal bank so as not to offend royal eyes – the newly confident planners were quite specific as to what had to be provided. In February 1991 Les Sparks was appointed director of planning and architecture; he then re-organised the department, bringing in a team of urban designers for the first time. Sparks was willing to see the proportion of offices increase, as long as the essentials of the scheme were retained: housing (reflecting a new policy of bringing people back into the city centre); restaurants and bars opposite the ICC; a 'people attractor' of some kind; a central square; and canal-side frontages and bridges.

Another new element entered the picture in 1991, the community planning group Birmingham for People, which had made an impact in the debate on the Bull Ring redevelopment with its 'People's Plan' alternative. In May BfP put on exhibition its own proposals for Brindleyplace. The emphasis was on mixed use, with fewer offices, high permeability, good pedestrian connections and well-designed public space. Apart from the canalside public park advocated by BfP, there was actually little distance between the positions of Birmingham for People, Rosehaugh and the city council – the definitions of good urban design were converging –

The completed Symphony Hall, home of the City of Birmingham Symphony Orchestra, and (below) the International Conference Centre (ICC) complex under construction in 1989 to the designs of PTP and RHWL. Oozells Street School (now the Ikon Gallery) and part of the Brindleyplace site are shown in the bottom right-hand corner. Fronting the ICC and Symphony Hall is Centenary Square, with paving designed by artist Tess Jaray (bottom).

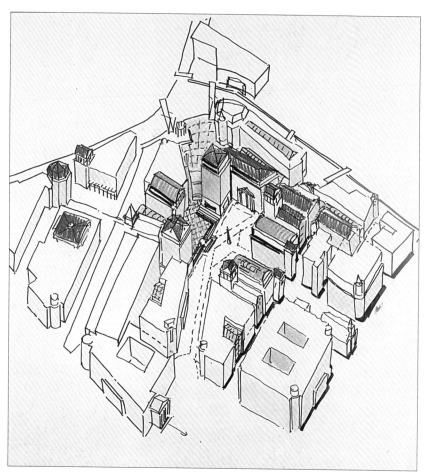

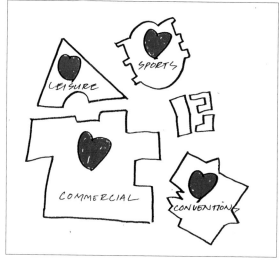

but the pressure group's intervention increased the expectations put upon the site.

A revised masterplan was produced in December 1991 and submitted for outline planning approval. The mall had now disappeared, replaced by the Water's Edge bar and restaurant scheme. Housing faced onto the canal, combined with other uses. Outline planning approval was granted in June 1992 with detailed approval for the Water's Edge. The basis of the outline approval was that the strategic principles of the masterplan – the central square, building footprints, pedestrian network, a minimum of 120 dwellings – were fixed but that everything else was illustrative. Each time an element was changed, there had to be a revised masterplan submitted for approval. Every part always had to be seen in context.

There was some concern inside the planning committee about whether the plan, no matter how good, could actually give rise to a lively, populated area. Unwisely Rosehaugh had taken the committee on a Sunday visit to a deserted Broadgate. As a result, the Terry Farrell Partnership commissioned Professor Bill Hillier, creator of the 'space syntax' method of urban analysis, to forecast pedestrian flows in Brindleyplace. This seems to have had the desired effect, although John Chatwin, then at Farrell's, doubts whether any of the elected

members actually understood the Hillier report. The one specific recommendation that it made was relocating the bridge over the canal from the ICC, making it axial with the ICC mall. This now seems obvious although it did not seem so at the time.

After years of uncertainty it seemed that progress was now in sight. But in November 1992 financial crisis hit Rosehaugh; the banks were withdrawing credit from the company as its debts mounted. Brindleyplace plc was by this time a wholly owned subsidiary of Rosehaugh. The site itself was owned by Brindleyplace plc on a 150-year lease from the city which imposed various development obligations (some of them time-related) and which could be terminated if these obligations were not met. If Brindleyplace plc went into full receivership the lease could also be terminated.

In November 1992 Rosehaugh went into receivership. Just hours before this happened, Chatham persuaded the chair of the planning committee to revise the lease, extending the timescale and allowing Brindleyplace plc to be kept afloat by the receivers long enough for a purchaser to be found. Chatham and Wright also persuaded the receivers of Rosehaugh to do just that and Brindleyplace plc was offered to the market, along with the site, tax losses and planning consent.

There were five bidders for the company; the bid

Terry Farrell Partnership's 1991
Brindleyplace masterplan for Rosehaugh:
concept drawings (left), model and
study of public open spaces (bottom).

by the developer Argent was not the highest but it demonstrated that it was able to perform quickly. In May 1993 it paid £3m, which would increase within a year to almost £8m with the development obligations imposed by the head-lease. Although it had not previously carried out a multi-building development project, Argent knew about masterplanning, having earlier worked with Edward Cullinan on proposals for the Morrison Street goods yard in Edinburgh. At Brindleyplace Argent saw the first task as revising the masterplan in line with its commercial strategy. To this end it appointed as masterplanner John Chatwin, who had previously been a partner at the Terry Farrell Partnership but was now an independent consultant.

Brindleyplace had survived difficult years in which little progress had been made. It had now entered calmer waters with the team who would turn it into a success.

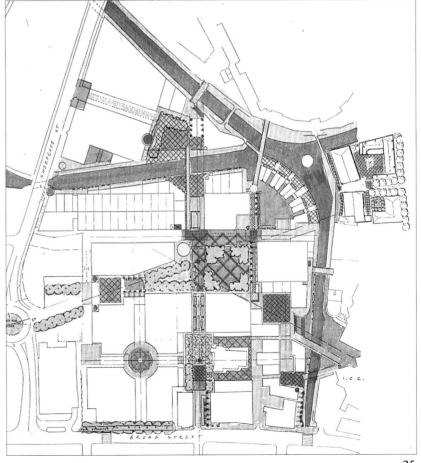

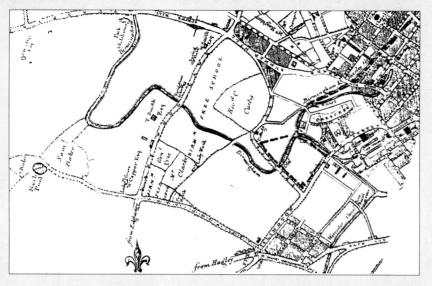

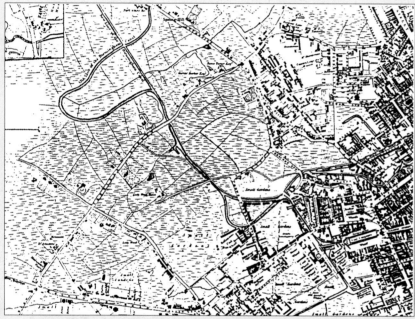

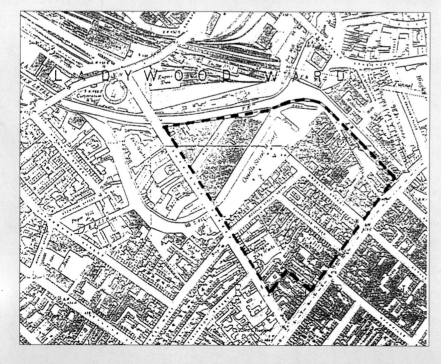

Chapter three: The Brindleyplace masterplan

John Chatwin

As a child growing up in Edgbaston, I remember Broad Street as a local shopping street containing a baker and grocer as well as a violin-maker and other specialist shops. At its western end, Five Ways was an elegant conjunction of urban streets celebrating the shift from commercial activity to mixed residential; Edgbaston and Ladywood were integrated communities. At its eastern end, Paradise Circus was still a real place, marking the entrance to the city centre, and containing the Woodman, a fine Edwardian pub where I was to spend many evenings as a student. Both these significant but subtle linkages were destroyed by building the inner ring road.

When I was 12, I discovered a small gate in Gas Street which led me to explore the canal system. The arteries that provided the lifeblood of the rapidly expanding Victorian city were a secret world, standing four metres below street level and enclosed by tall brick buildings. In 1768 James Brindley built the Birmingham Canal to bring coal and metals from the Black Country; it followed the contours to make the elegant curve now known as the Brindley Loop. With the growth of the canal system, manufacturing buildings were built along the canal to the north of Broad Street: brass foundries, tube rolling mills, button and glass works. In 1827 the Brindley Loop was by-passed by Telford's realignment of the canal, which now forms the northern edge of Brindleyplace. At this date, the area between the canal and Sheepcote Street was still undeveloped. By 1900, the Ordnance Survey shows the entire Brindleyplace site developed with commercial buildings along the canal and Oozells Street and a mixture of densely packed small-scale residential buildings closer to Broad Street.

Such was the origin of the site, largely cleared of buildings, that was acquired by Argent in May 1993. In August I was appointed to review the development, prepare a revised masterplan and assist in re-negotiating the phasing and other requirements. In line with the Highbury Initiative, the overall aim was to create an active and welcoming new quarter that would be a natural extension to the fabric of the city, restoring the links and connections that had been destroyed by the inner ring road and other planning policies of the 60s and 70s.

Although based on the 1991 Farrell masterplan (on which I had worked) the 1993 masterplan differed in significant respects. These included:
• adjustments to the development plot layouts to provide greater flexibility for a variety of building forms (for example, less reliance on large-floorplate Broadgate-style office buildings);
• revisions to vehicular circulation so that arrival and drop-off by car and taxi became central to the identity and use of the whole development;
• revisions to the pedestrian circulation in response to changes to surrounding sites and proposals for public transport;
• providing an opportunity for implementation of the housing earlier and as a whole, rather than piecemeal and over different plots;
• giving a more prominent location to the leisure element;
• giving greater emphasis to the main public spaces as a framework for the development.

The masterplan also had to be capable of an almost infinite variety of phasing while being comprehensible and workable at each stage during construction. In December 1993 the revised masterplan was presented to and accepted by the city planning committee; revised masterplan principles, vehicle circulation, disposition of uses and indicative plot drawings (and resulting development obligations) were then substituted within the development agreement. This documentation required the masterplan to be reviewed and updated from time to time as the development proceeded; with this proviso, the design of individual buildings was then dealt with as submission of reserved matters in pursuance to the outline planning permission.

There were a number of specific objectives:
• to integrate into the west end of Birmingham 1.1 million square feet (102,300 square metres) of high-quality modern office space in eight to ten separate buildings. The provision of a major public open space (the fifth in a sequence now defining the city centre) as well as retail, leisure, cultural and residential buildings was a fundamental part of creating a new quarter which would be active well into the evening and at weekends.
• to provide an urban framework for the design of a set of buildings, each designed by leading architects, that are related to each other and to their larger context but which combine to create a sense of place and clear identity for Brindleyplace.

Development of Ladywood: c1800, c1850 and c1900. Although Broad Street is an ancient ridge route linking the original Georgian hill town of Birmingham with the manor of Edgbaston, the area now occupied by Brindleyplace and the International Convention Centre was essentially rural until well after the building of the canals in the second half of the eighteenth century. Redeveloped for the first time in the 1990s as a result of substantial public and private investment, it is now the focal point of the westward expansion of the revitalised city centre.

• to provide a flexible arrangement of serviced plots which could be developed with buildings which are efficient and flexible for tenants, healthy and safe for occupiers, welcoming and responsive to adjacent public spaces and readily accessible from the transport network while offering the highest on-plot and visitor parking provision in the city.

• to provide a cohesive group of buildings and spaces, as a natural extension of the existing fabric of the city, which relate to neighbouring developments and form links with adjacent communities.

• to enhance the appreciation and use of the canal system by visitors to the International Convention Centre and Symphony Hall and other business tourists, as well as by the people of Birmingham, whether as users of the retail and entertainment elements of the development or as visitors, cyclists or joggers!

Implementation of the masterplan involved unusually close collaboration between the developer's design team and the planning authority. A series of masterplan meetings were held throughout the process; outline proposals for individual sites were considered by all interested parties prior to detail design or any formal planning application. The masterplan was constantly reviewed and adjusted to ensure that proposals for individual elements did not frustrate achievement of the urban objectives for the whole site and the city's aspirations for the new quarter.

While the purchase agreement required the main square only to be simply demarcated (and temporarily landscaped) before any building was let, Argent understood that an initial major investment in fully completing the square was necessary to establish a sense of place and clear identity for Brindleyplace. The presence of a completed public space at the centre of a large and complex building site posed considerable construction sequence and logistical constraints. Temporary surface parking and builder's compounds were organised so that pedestrian routes were created through the square from the outset, helping to shape public understanding of the orientation of the spaces.

A major landscape and infrastructure contract of £2.5 million, which greatly exceeded the developer's liabilities under their agreement with the city, started on site in April 1994 and was completed in

Located adjacent to Broad Street between the city centre and the middle ring road, Brindleyplace (shown in red) is connected to the city centre across the (sunken) inner ring road.

Traffic planning

Aidan Hughes

The main principle of traffic planning at Brindleyplace is to accommodate motor cars and goods vehicles but not allow this to lead the design, *writes Aidan Hughes of Ove Arup & Partners*. Pedestrians can walk without fear of speeding traffic and large areas are totally traffic-free; yet, when completed,

there will be 2,600 parking spaces as well as service deliveries to some 20 locations.

Some may query the lack of obvious kerb lines, the minimal number of signs and the intrusion of an occasional vehicle loading from the street, but these decisions were taken deliberately: we wanted to create an environment, not just a road or a service area. There were many trade-offs but we always believed that a driver would respond to the quality of the environment by driving slowly and with sensitivity. And the environment wasn't created just by the roads but by the buildings, the activity and the landscaping.

As with all masterplans,

commercial reality has required changes to be made but the principles have survived. The most obvious is that service vehicles are kept away from other traffic and from pedestrian 'desire-lines' and pedestrian areas. Less obvious is the way that cars are led to both the multi-storey and the underground car parks by direct routes, with minimal opportunity for conflict. This has been achieved without one-way streets and without undue concern that at times some vehicles will need to use the full road width. Indeed, the inclusion of such 'conflicts' is entirely consistent with the low-speed, shared-surface philosophy.

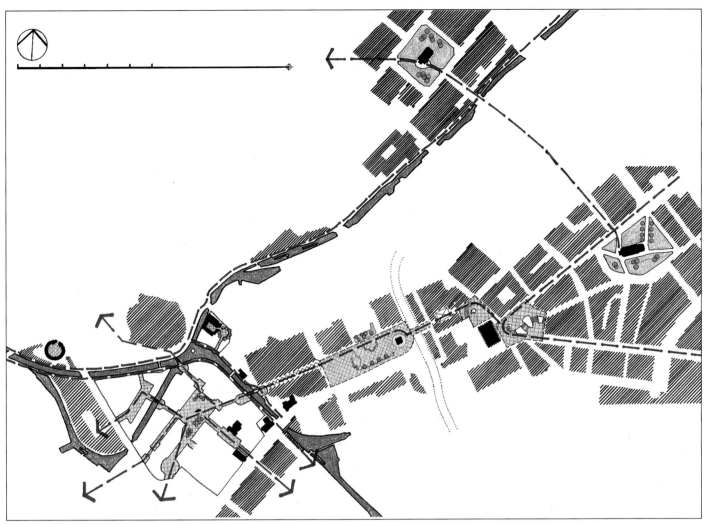

A pedestrian route from the city centre leads east to west from Victoria Square through Chamberlain Square and Centenary Square to Brindleyplace.

Ground contamination

Keith Jones

The investigation and development work carried out at Brindleyplace has dealt with contamination from 200 years of industrial use, *writes Keith Jones of RPS Consultants.* The result has been to effectively eliminate risks of environmental harm and regulatory or third party liabilities.

The Brindleyplace site has a long and complex industrial history dating back to about 1780, when a brass works was erected on the site by the Birmingham Metal Company. By the mid-nineteenth century, it had become an area of diverse industries, many related to the manufacture of brass and other metals, as well as other manufacturing trades related to the canal. The site was used into the 1970s and 80s but by 1991 it had been largely cleared.

There was potential for contamination anywhere on the site, but there were particular areas, such as filled-in canal basins, locations of brass works and former areas of open ground, where the risk was greatest. From 1991 a series of investigations was carried out across the site, continuing as individual plots were developed. These showed widespread contamination with zinc and copper (the components of brass) within made ground and also sporadic contamination with other heavy metals, sulphate and mineral oil. The made ground was typically between one and three metres thick but in some areas extended to over seven metres. Beneath the made ground were shallow drift deposits of glacial sand and gravel and below this the base of Wildmoor (Bromsgrove) sandstone.

The ground contamination did not generally present a risk to hard-surfaced commercial development; so in areas where excavation was not necessary for construction purposes, the made ground has been left in situ. Before development of each plot, a detailed geotechnical and environmental site investigation was carried out. Remediation requirements were assessed on the basis of a method statement setting out Argent's requirements. On completion of the groundworks for each plot, the contractor was required to prepare a report describing the works carried out and the results of verification testing.

Development of most of the office buildings required deep excavations in order to construct basements, the buildings being founded in natural sandstone. This has resulted in the removal of the major part of the contaminated material. Made ground remains beneath the site infrastructure and public squares and, to a limited extent, beneath some buildings such as the Crescent Theatre. To facilitate the sale and/or letting of buildings, comprehensive documentation was compiled, including environmental reviews of ground conditions and remedial work, plus all site investigation reports, method statements and contractors' remediation reports.

29

advance of any office building. This included new vehicular access from Sheepcote Street to serve the whole site (except the Water's Edge, which is serviced from Broad Street) as well as complete hard and soft landscape to the main square. Townshend Landscape Architects was appointed to design the main square plus the hard and soft landscape works.

An enclosed square, directly off Sheepcote Street, marks the point of arrival for all vehicles. A short road then connects to a tree-filled orientation space, as an annexe to the main square, which provides taxi drop-off, disabled parking and main vehicle circulation to individual buildings and the multi-storey car park. The raised area of the main square (which has pedestrian connections to the ICC and Broad Street) is substantially paved and contains an informal amphitheatre as well as raised and sloping grass areas. A hierarchy of materials defines the areas specifically for vehicles, areas of shared use and the main spaces predominantly used by pedestrians. Natural stone and sealed gravel, cobbles reclaimed from the site and mature specimen trees have been used throughout.

Early in the masterplanning process, it was agreed that the conceptual design for the four office buildings around the main square should be developed in parallel with the preparation of detailed designs for the layout landscape of the square. Urban design guidelines and other technical briefing requirements were therefore prepared for this group of buildings. Whilst defining overall footprint, general massing and required building lines, these guidelines were as non-prescriptive as possible, with emphasis on the spirit rather than the letter of the requirements. During this process, five group design presentations and discussions were held with all the architects (and usually the city planners) so that specific relationships between individual buildings could be established and a common approach to materials, height, massing and linkages could evolve, rather than being imposed on each architect. Ove Arup & Partners was involved with the development of conceptual designs for all buildings, so that common attitudes to structure, energy efficiency and fire engineering could be adopted; Silk & Frazier was available for cost advice. Architects for each plot were selected from a shortlist drawn up after a review of work and

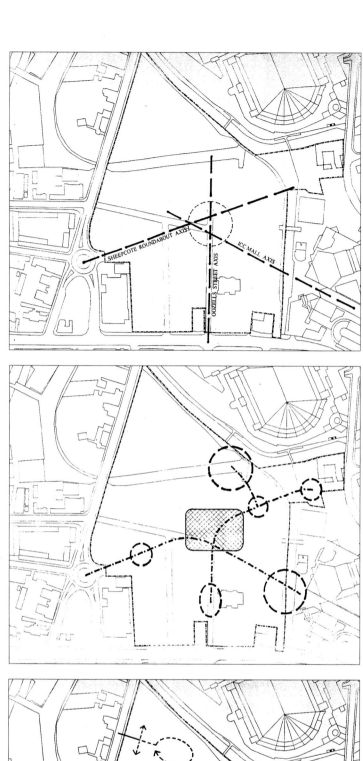

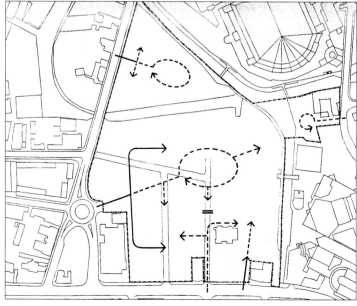

URBAN DESIGN

ANALYSIS OF MASSING & AXES

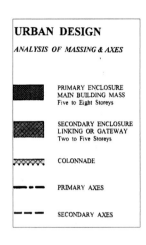

PRIMARY ENCLOSURE
MAIN BUILDING MASS
Five to Eight Storeys

SECONDARY ENCLOSURE
LINKING OR GATEWAY
Two to Five Storeys

COLONNADE

PRIMARY AXES

SECONDARY AXES

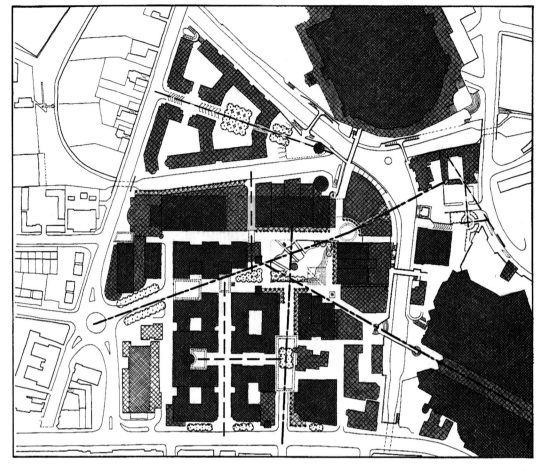

MASTERPLAN ACTIVITY

SHOWING PUBLIC OPEN SPACES;
RETAIL, PUBS & RESTAURANTS;
LEISURE; RELOCATED THEATRE;
POSSIBLE GALLERY & ATRIA

MAIN PUBLIC SPACES

ACTIVITY USES

OFFICE ATRIA

Analysis of massing/axes and public
spaces in the 1993 masterplan.
Opposite: principal axes, linked open
spaces and vehicular access.

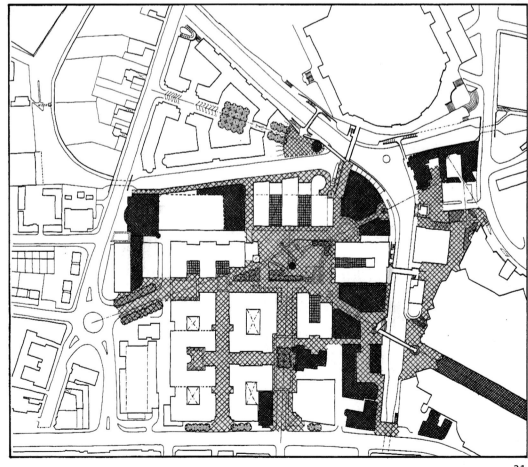

1993
As part of the headlease obligation imposed on us by Birmingham city council, Argent was required to develop the Water's Edge speculatively and refurbish Oozells Street School. For this we used our own money entirely.

1994
With units in the Water's Edge starting to let, we agreed to sell the end investment to British Airways Pension Trustees on the basis that they forward-funded the speculative construction of Number One.

1995
Site sales, all with development obligations, to Berkeley Homes, Greenalls and the Institute of Electrical Engineers enabled us to finance the construction of the central square and main site infrastructure. Berkeley Homes (now Crosby Homes) started construction of housing on the triangle site in January 1995. The listed Kingston Building was restored by the Institute of Electrical Engineers as a conference centre and on the adjacent Brewers Dock Greenalls built a new public house.

interview; the main criterion was a particular approach or design skill appropriate to urban concerns implicit in particular parts of the site. Commonality of style was deliberately not an issue; a commitment to design excellence and thereby a mutual respect – so that each could work as part of a cohesive team – was. Our cities gain strength from variety; uniformity of style stultifies and highlights the boundaries within which 'planners have been at work'. The idea is that, in time, the edges of Brindleyplace will become increasingly indistinct.

The two squares are carefully related spatially; they complement each other in use and character. The central square establishes the identity of Brindleyplace and also provides the address on which the economics of the development are founded; it is a business place and a thoroughfare within the context of the city. Although it contains retail and restaurant uses, Oozells Square is more contemplative; it is linked to other spaces – both visually and organisationally – and thus generates two additional routes to Broad Street. The configuration of this second square provides a proper setting for the fine listed school building – already restored by Argent as part of the initial infrastructure – which has now been converted to provide the new Ikon Gallery.

Rather than choose art works – or even specific locations – a shortlist of artists was invited to make wide-ranging proposals responding to the whole of the public spaces. The selected sculptor, Miles Davies, made three works: a large central piece that included an intervention in the paving of the square and two related pieces marking entrances to the development. Paul de Monchaux was fully involved in the detail design of Oozells Square, the second public space; his sculptures double as seats and ceremonial arches which contribute to the tranquil atmosphere achieved in this part of the site.

A study for the enhancement of Broad Street was also undertaken, in conjunction with the Broad Street Association, covering the area between Five Ways (ie the middle ring road) and Centenary Square (inner ring road). As well as consultation with major owners, occupiers, businesses and residents, this involved analysis of pedestrian and traffic usage and also of wind turbulence and other environmental problems. A number of strategies were

Planning for the market

Roger Madelin

Since the recession of the early 90s, finance to build speculatively has been difficult to obtain, *writes Roger Madelin of Argent*. We therefore had to plan Brindleyplace so that it could be taken forward stage by stage, as and when money was available. We could not predict the sequence of building and so our masterplan had to allow for the maximum number of possible sequences.

The 17 acre (6.9 hectare) site which we purchased in May 1993 had been assembled by the city council largely as a by-product of the creation of the International Convention Centre and National Indoor Arena. It was then sold on the open market

to a consortium which subsequently ran into difficulties. Control then passed to Rosehaugh who secured planning consent for a mixed commercial and leisure/residential scheme masterplanned by Terry Farrell. This comprised 1.1 million square feet (102,300 square metres) of offices, 330,000 square feet (30,700 square metres) of shops, restaurants and pubs; two hotels; a site for cinema or other leisure uses; 120 houses and 2,600 car parking spaces. But towards the end of 1992 Rosehaugh went into receivership.

Argent paid the receivers £3m for the site. At the time this was considered a large sum to pay for 17 acres of wasteland to the west of the city centre. The S106 planning obligation required the owner of the long leasehold of the site to build the first 60,000 square feet (5,600 square metres) of retail/restaurants speculatively, refurbish a derelict grade 2 listed school and lay out the main square. The expenditure we faced

before enjoying any income was therefore nearer to £8m.

The masterplan consent had a good mix of uses. To enable us to make some return on our investment, surely one of the uses could generate a return or some cash back? The market for property and for finance in 1993 was close to dead but we knew that 'what goes down must come up' – but when and in which sector?

In our view, the masterplan consent that we inherited was more suited to an all-in-one-go development than to the step-by-step approach that we envisaged. We therefore had to revise the masterplan to allow any one of the permitted uses to proceed as the market allowed. As and when the first element produced a return, we would be able to put that money back into the scheme, facilitating the remaining elements.

A good masterplan must pass a 'what if' phasing test. Our revised masterplan did and has proved its value.

1996

Pre-letting 120,000 square feet (11,200 square metres) to BT enabled us to develop Number Five.

1996

Site sales with development obligations to Vardon allowed the National Sealife Centre to go ahead. A pre-let to Lloyds TSB allowed Number Two to be developed. Oozells Street School was 'given' by us to the Ikon Gallery with a sum of money, on the condition they could obtain Lottery and European Regional Development Fund finance.

1997

Argent Development Consortium was formed, comprising Argent Group plc, British Telecom Pension Scheme, Citibank and UBK with a loan from a consortium of German banks. This enabled us to build speculatively two office buildings, the multi-storey car park and new Crescent Theatre. To spread the risk of developing speculatively, Argent's Thames Valley Park near Reading and Governor's House in the City of London were also included in the consortium.

1998

The successful letting and sale of Number Three allowed the consortium to press ahead with the speculative development of Oozells Square and Numbers Nine and Six.

1999

A site sale with development obligations will allow the hotel to proceed. The successful letting and sales of any of the current speculative buildings, or pre-lettings, will allow the progressive development of Numbers Seven, Eight and Ten.

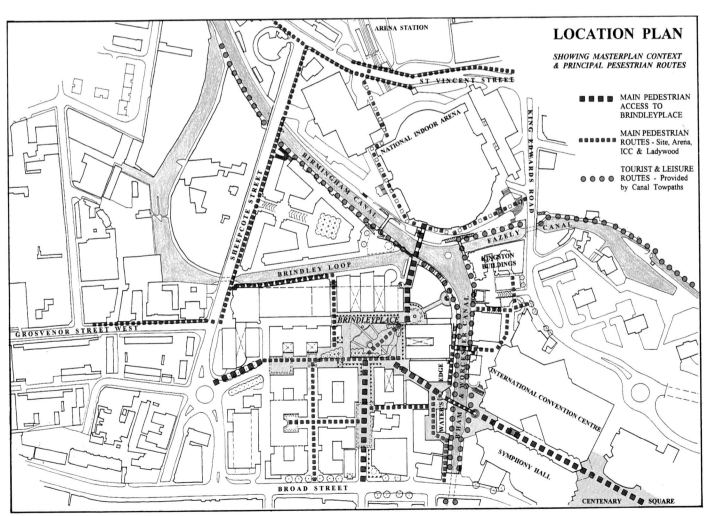

examined with a view to enhancing pedestrian activity, facilitating vehicle access for users and service while discouraging through traffic, revitalising traditional retail and leisure uses, reducing the perceived barrier presented by the street and encouraging the development of community links. The aim was that Broad Street should again become the focal point of a mixed residential and business community rather than the boundary between two separate neighbourhoods. The first phase, funded by the European Regional Development Fund, has been completed, comprising wider pavements, traffic calming, addditional pedestrian crossing points and enhanced street furniture.

Of course no single development, however large, can resolve problems originating on a city scale. But by providing the essential mix of urban paraphernalia – including streets, squares, bars, cafes, people, employment and activity – Brindleyplace helps subsume the monocultural giants of the International Convention Centre and National Indoor Arena within the real stuff of which cities are made. While access problems associated with downgrading the inner ring road remain to be fully solved by first class public transport, connections have been re-established and Broad Street and its hinterland can make a vibrant contribution to the life of the city.

Working with the masterplan

Graham Morrison

In both the buildings that Allies & Morrison has designed at Brindleyplace, Number Two and Number Six, the masterplan has been effective in provoking a particular response. The context is rich in pattern, scale and connections and a masterplan was needed which would not only acknowledge the commercial imperative of the development but also effect continuity within the city while allowing an individuality for each separate site. The early decision to find a loose and informal arrangement within a strong landscape and avoid an overall design from a single architect was clearly the right one.

Each building has a series of different determinants which demand distinct responses in relation to hierarchy, scale, material, and composition. The underlying asymmetry has helped create a sense of uncontrived variety while facilitating construction (and ultimately reconstruction) over a period of time. The focus is always on the place and not the building, the whole and not the part. It is not an 'ideal city' as one might experience through the eyes of Piero della Francesca; rather it is continuous with Birmingham and its vibrant commercial activity.

The dominance of brick as a facing material has ensured an overall visual unity, broken only at significant points within the site to signal axis, vista, and entrance. The tripartite elevational division has allowed the base level to establish a particular relationship to the immediate outside space, the middle level to effect continuity of enclosure to the squares, and the top of each of the buildings to provide a varied silhouette.

Demetri Porphyrios

The masterplan provides the scaffold and the idiosyncracies of the buildings furnish the infill. This has always been the working hypothesis of the traditional city and it is this principle that the Brindleyplace masterplan adopts. Designed by different architects, the office buildings, shops, restaurants, housing and leisure buildings respond to the urban pattern of streets which converge around two public squares and the canal front.

The masterplan must always aspire to a setting for a life both productive and pleasurable. This present-day humanism takes from the ancients the essential definition of 'disegno' as shown in the idea of urban design.

Urban design configures the ideal in a disegno for reality to approximate. The disegno never exists as an empirical reality. It is a paradigm that guides without curtailing interpretative freedom and it becomes a real city-plan only when it is interpreted under pressures of everyday life.

It was in that spirit that Porphyrios Associates addressed the Brindleyplace masterplan. It suggested where the front entrance to our building should be, how the arcade embraces the square, the advancing and the receding volumes of our building's massing, the height for its main cornice and the scale of its formal elements.

In turn, our building gave the masterplan the bones and flesh it needed if it were to sustain itself as an urban design idea. Such is the dialogue always between architecture and the city.

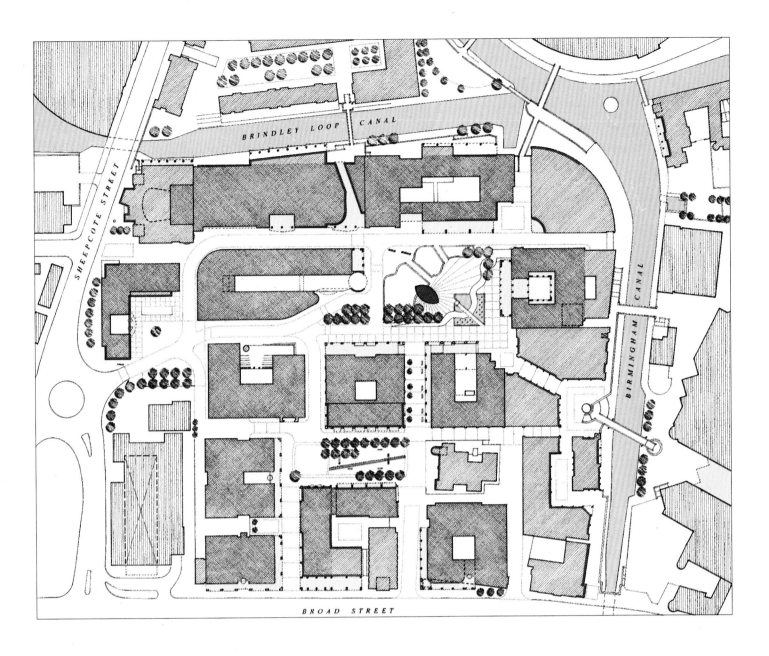

The masterplan as at July 1999 and
(below) preliminary survey for Broad
Street enhancement proposals.

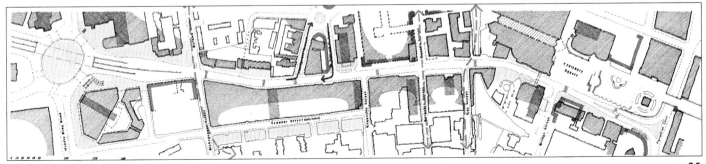

Chapter four: Turning ideas into reality

Roger Madelin

On a bright May morning in 1993, we were standing in the middle of 17 acres (6.9 hectares) of wasteland, *writes Roger Madelin of Argent.* Although it was derelict, we knew that such a site, with planning consent and vacant possession in a single ownership in a major city, was an opportunity of a lifetime. We all knew that we had to create the very best that was achievable. No doubt this sounds far too visionary – and benevolent – for a developer but we really felt that way… and still do. With such a large site, and so many buildings with different uses, we were determined to work with the best designers and builders and to choose those who could work well together and inspire and learn from each other.

Our business plan was prepared using three scenarios for the level of market demand, low, medium and high. We had to finance for the possibility of the worst case but prepare our management structure and project planning for the best. This envisaged completing the scheme in seven years, which would mean placing over 25 building contracts and spending £200m on construction – a construction expenditure of over £100,000 every working day.

Argent's business as a developer is not construction but construction plays a major part in our business. When we enter into a construction contract, we want certainty – certainty of quality, price and time, certainty that the contractor will still be there in 12 years time and certainty that we can respond positively to changing requirements.

We have never understood why most procurers of buildings allow design to be separated from construction. No other industry would ignore, for the larger part of the process, both the manufacturer and specialists who are to deliver a unique product. Yet so often they are presented with the design as a fait accompli. We also cannot understand why so many clients still believe in tendering work to six firms of contractors; they seem to ignore the costs of going through the same learning curve every time. In contrast, Argent has always involved the people who are going to procure and assemble the building and the specialist suppliers and contractors from the start of the design process. We believe that this is the only way to ensure that our buildings are delivered at market cost or less.

At Brindleyplace we met with six contractors, chosen by their balance sheets and reputations (we had already worked with three of them). Business objectives were openly discussed – how could each of us add value and increase profits? Our requirement was for certainty. All agreed that the right answer was design & build fixed-price contracts, but with enough time for designer and contractor to develop and understand the product we wanted. Evaluation, innovation and value engineering were the ways to keep the cost down. We agreed not to tender if we could benchmark costs and beat the market rate.

All six contractors showed themselves skilled and enthusiastic. We had agreed, however, that only two should be asked to tender the first office building (no-one could benchmark the costs for offices in early 1994, because none had been built for some years!). We were very impressed with the quality of the bids by Wimpey (now Tarmac) and Kyle Stewart (now HBG) and chose them. Wimpey won the tender and started building Number One in June 1994.

Since then we have not tendered any major project and have worked with Tarmac and HBG on most of Brindleyplace. The exceptions were Tilbury Douglas (Water's Edge, main square and Oozells Street School) and Norwest Holst (car park and Crescent Theatre). By setting tough targets and benchmarking, we are confident that costs have been at or below market rates while safety, quality and programme have been second to none.

The design and construction teams, including the specialist subcontractors, work together from sketch concept design onwards. Every element is benchmarked to ensure that we are at or below market cost. A fee is paid to the contractor and to the specialist if the lead-in process is long or there is a risk that the project may not happen. A fixed-price, all-risks design & build contract is entered into before construction commences on site.

It can take up to a year to design each building, achieve discharge of reserved planning matters and enter into a fixed-price contract. To be ready to start the next building when the market is right, therefore, involves forward thinking. Not knowing which building the market wants next also means that we have to keep our options open. Designing a building ready to start construction costs a great deal of money and, as the market may require that building to change, we have had to push ahead just far enough, usually to obtain planning consent.

Perspective renderings by Jock Bevan showing Brindleyplace viewed from, and towards the direction of, the city centre.

37

Partnering in practice

Kevin Hole

The introduction of Argent to Brindleyplace was an eye-opener, *writes Kevin Hole of Silk & Frazier.* Concern for the wellbeing of contractors and the desire to avoid abortive tendering costs was not unknown but Argent's enthusiasm for such principles was different. It soon became clear that we would be asked to 'boldly go where no contract had gone before' – even Latham hadn't got there yet.

The concept of partnering was rapidly embraced, together with the recognition that the benefits of partnering have to be actively sought. Partnering doesn't just happen: considerable effort is required to extract its benefits. This principle was driven into the core of the Brindleyplace process. But partnering as a concept relies heavily upon trust, which in turn can only exist through mutual respect.

Notwithstanding their enthusiasm for partnering, Argent were relatively unfamiliar with the midlands' construction market and so the first office contract, for Number One, was let in a limited competitive environment. The two-stage tender process commenced with six contractors. From this Wimpey Construction (now Tarmac Construction) and Kyle Stewart (now HBG Construction) were selected to submit full design & build tenders.

The prices were close and the submissions impressive. Both teams were likeable and appeared trustworthy. The decision came down to cost and the contract was awarded to Wimpey. But the process had identified much more than a successful contractor for the first office building: it had uncovered two potential partners for the remainder of the site.

So partnering at Brindleyplace was born. In the event Wimpey (Tarmac Construction) was awarded Numbers One, Two, Four and Six Brindleyplace, while Kyle Stewart (HBG) took Numbers Three, Five, Seven and Nine plus the cafe. But partnering should never override the importance of selecting partners with the necessary experience for a project and for this reason Norwest Holst, being experts in car park construction, were introduced for the multi-storey car park and this led on to their appointment for the adjoining Crescent Theatre.

The early partnering projects were subjected to a vigorous but logical development process made up of ten steps (opposite).

Partnering should not be seen as a panacea for all ills in the construction industry. Unlike manufacturing or factory production, every construction project is different, with particular problems and challenges. At Silk & Frazier, partnering has been described as 'mutual massaging'. It eases the aches and pains experienced in traditional contracts but does not necessary eliminate them. The aim is to minimise pain by anticipation through preparation – and preparation can take place only if the right

As with all the office buildings at Brindleyplace, the frame of Number Nine is wrapped in brick elevations.

team is assembled early enough, as at Brindleyplace. The mutual massaging approach encourages each party to massage someone else's problem, rather than ignoring it. So often, the hunt for the scapegoat causes parties to retract into a contractual shell. We have encouraged honesty without reprisal, which ultimately leads to resolution before pain leads to terminal illness.

The experience of Brindleyplace has shown that, for the process of partnering to be a success, each member has to feel involved. Each party has to have a feeling of ownership in the project. This is harder to achieve than one might think. The only way ownership can be achieved is through sharing. The principle of sharing has run though the projects as a core requirement. It has been achieved in the key areas of design, cost plan, workshops and savings.

The success of any relationship is measured by its product and satisfaction. No contract sum at Brindleyplace has exceeded the cost plan set for the project. No final account agreement has exceeded Argent's budget. No claim has been received and no major delays have been experienced.

Maybe this would have been the case anyway but I suspect that partnering is the main reason for this success. As Dr Spock would have said, 'it's a job, Jim, but not as we know it'.

Step 1 – Appointment of a concept team

The architectural philosophy at Brindleyplace has been to establish buildings of individual note designed by well-known and highly regarded architectural practices. While being individual, the buildings were to be complementary in an urban environment. To this end early concept designs were established with a team comprising architect, structural and m&e engineers and quantity surveyor, who collectively would become employer's agent. This team was allowed to 'play' with the scheme to increase efficiency and to explore innovative ideas. The contracts would be design & build but without the concept team being novated to the contractor.

Step 2 – Presentation to the contactor

Once the concept design and cost plan had been produced, the chosen contractor was called to a presentation. The scheme was presented and perceived problems and difficulties were outlined. The cost plan was handed to the contractor for his comment.

Step 3 – Contractor presentation to client

The contractor was invited to respond to the concept design and to comment on improvements, resolutions and areas of risk. An outline programme and method statement was presented and discussed. The cost plan was responded to which allowed, with some ensuing discussions, joint ownership to be taken of it.

Step 4 – Value engineering

Value engineering then took place, as necessary, to bring the cost plan in line with the set budget.

Step 5 – Subcontractor partnering

It was not unusual for subcontractors to have a significant input on the design. Too often in projects, good ideas from subcontractors cannot be adopted because irreversible decisions preventing their implementation have already been made. It was therefore decided that it would be prudent for certain key packages to be partnered, thus allowing their expertise to be brought into the process early.

Step 6 – Detailed design

With a separate design team appointed by the contractor, there was the opportunity to 'share' design development with the concept team, avoiding duplication and permitting cross-fertilisation of ideas. The early involvement of subcontractor designs allowed many uncertainties to be ironed out and the efficiency of the design to be maximised. The construction team constantly monitored buildability and the suitability of material selection. The early assembling of the full team also allowed a proper consideration of green issues, low maintenance options and life cycle costs.

Step 7 – Partnering workshop

This was held before commencement on site but towards the end of the pre-contract period and provided an opportunity to take stock, review and to formulate ways forward. A comfortable location away from the office environment was used for the workshop.

Step 8 – Agreement of contract sum

A fixed-price, all-risk lump sum was agreed with the contractor, using open-book negotiation. The lump sum includes an agreed contractor's design development allowance, giving sufficient funds to finalise any details not yet agreed or resolved.

Step 9 – Construction

Simple really, build it! The concept design team is retained to comment on the detailed design as it develops.

Step 10 – Review

It is imperative that the process and its inherent procedures are constantly reviewed and remedial action taken promptly when problems are identified.

Building services

Mark Facer

The building services at Brindleyplace are designed to meet the expectations of potential tenants while respecting the ideal of sustainable city centre development, *writes Mark Facer of Ove Arup & Partners*. The main facade materials are brick and clear glass. Window sizes are limited, with consequent benefits to solar gains, comfort and running costs. The internal standards for safety, temperature, lighting, power and fresh air are designed to meet or exceed the requirements of modern tenants.

The first office, Number One, is on the relatively noisy Broad Street and so is air-conditioned, with a four-pipe fan coil unit system enhanced to suit anticipated market requirements. In designing subsequent office buildings in the quieter heart of the development, early consideration was given to natural ventilation and so most of the buildings are planned with a maximum of 13.5 metres from outside wall to atrium. While natural ventilation is a possibility,

at present the vast majority of potential tenants require air-conditioned offices and most of the buildings therefore incorporate fan coil unit air conditioning systems.

But where appropriate the opportunity has been taken to implement alternative methods. For example Number Five was pre-let to BT and this allowed the skin of the building to be fine-tuned to give an enhanced environmental performance. It was therefore possible for the air conditioning system to be extremely simple and it is all the more effective for that. Air at 18°C is supplied via circular floor grilles through a 400mm deep floor void, which is uncluttered by anything other than communication and power cables. Vitiated air is passed back to air handling plant on the roof through the ceiling void. Encouraged by Number Five, Argent decided to develop Number Four on a speculative basis with enough space in floor and ceiling voids for a similar system to be installed by future tenants.

Structural engineering

Richard Henley

The founding material at Brindleyplace is sandstone, *writes Richard Henley of Ove Arup & Partners*. In both its weathered and unweathered state this allows buildings to be constructed on simple concrete pads or strip footings. Most of the buildings have one- or two-storey basements for car parking and plant. A good number of the basement excavations have been carried right up to existing structures (either the canal, public highway or existing buildings). Generally, bored pile retaining walls have been used, with the walls constructed before the excavations are carried out; this limits movement of the adjacent ground during digging and allows excavations to be made close to existing structures.

Apart from the multi-storey car park, the building forms are not derived directly from structural systems. The car park uses a recently patented form of a warped surface (VCM) system that effectively creates an elongated flat spiral between the main up and

down ramps, significantly reducing their length. This allows more of the footprint of the building to be devoted to parking spaces, improving planning efficiency.

The form of the office buildings is largely derived from considerations of office layout and site plan. The primary function of the structure is to transmit the weight of people, equipment and its own weight safely to the foundations. It must also stand up to the wind. Sufficiently strong but flexible stability systems can cause various forms of buckling instability of the frames, whose task is to support the vertical gravity loads. The traditional location for stability systems is in and around stair and lift cores, which also provide the means of distributing services. In the quest for improved floor-plate planning efficiency, cores become smaller and are not always located in the most structurally efficient places, which for steel frame buildings can present a demanding challenge. Integrating services routes

with the stability structures in cores below a certain size or in an awkward location quickly shows that it is not feasible to put enough steel into a braced stability system to make it stiff enough. A sophistication at Brindleyplace has been to adapt a concept from high-rise steel framed buildings and use reinforced concrete for some of the core walls, exploiting its inherent stiffness.

The structure of Number Five takes advantage both of an under-floor air supply plenum and the plan of the building to create column-free office space, with long-span rolled-steel I-beams located in a ceiling void containing just lighting, fire alarm systems and the return air plenum.

The visual and tactile qualities of Numbers Two and Three result from using load-bearing brick walls. For both buildings the brick walls pass in front of the structural frames and are only restrained by them for wind load. By thoughtful design, these walls have been detailed with the minimum of movement joints.

Marketing Brindleyplace

Roger Madelin

Marketing has played a key role in turning Brindleyplace into reality, *writes Roger Madelin of Argent*. It falls into three areas: researching what the market wants; establishing and maintaining the Brindleyplace brand; and informing the market.

Researching the market

Developers are in the customer services sector. Our products – the buildings – have to be right for the market. They need to be right in terms of size, specification, quality and cost; they should provide the right flexibility; and, perhaps most important, they need to be available at the right time. But, for whatever reason, very few occupiers talk to us early enough in the process for us to design and deliver a building to meet their specific requirements.

Speculative development can pay a good dividend if the timing is right. Research into market supply and demand, historic trends and economic outlook can obviously help to produce the right building at the right time. Finding out all we could about the 16 million square feet (1.5 million square metres) of office stock in Birmingham city centre was an essential part of our research. Lease lengths, history of take-up, specification, inward investment and listening to occupiers' current concerns and future aspirations: these are all part of an information-gathering task that is taken very seriously. Since few of our potential customers wish to talk to us, creating an environment where we can learn what they want is a major part of this. To this end we have arranged various events including architectural presentations, urban design discussions, security seminars, small dinners with high-profile guest speakers and breakfast seminars.

One disappointment has been the almost complete lack of interest in the market in sustainability or energy-saving opportunities. No-one wants to be first. We have proposed a number of low-energy building solutions and green transport initiatives, but so far to no avail. We will keep trying.

Establishing the brand

For several years before we acquired Brindleyplace, the previous developer had been announcing, on a fairly regular basis, what was about to happen at Brindleyplace – but nothing happened. The first thing we needed to establish was credibility.

At our first press conference, a reporter asked when we were going to start building. Having held several meetings with the design and construction team, we could give a precise answer – 6th September. Our PR consultants, retained from the previous developer, cringed. But on 6th September the press and television crews were on site and so was our contractor – the construction of Brindleyplace had started. Since then we have always tried to be as good as our word.

Our research led us to design buildings for the Birmingham market with a number of distinctive features. These include clear glass (not tinted), with most windows openable; better natural light, using narrow floor widths (ie glass to glass) of 12 to 15 metres; a planning module of 1.5m; use of the external envelope as an environmental moderator; emphasis on good design (rather than marble and glitz) and on tried and tested materials; lower internal lighting levels (350-400 lux); a choice of environmental servicing, including mixed mode or low-energy options; bigger floor plates of 10-20,000 square feet (930-1860 square metres), with atria to provide natural light to the largest floor plates; and a single design and construction warranty from a substantial contractor. We believe that by working with some of the best architects and contractors in the UK we have been able to deliver a superior product. Quality of product is part of our brand.

Informing the market

This final part of our strategy involves marketing in the more traditional sense: informing the market of what we propose, what we are doing and what we have done. With some 20 different building projects completed and with already about 50 occupiers (excluding residents), there has been plenty to tell on a regular basis.

To inform a wide business audience, we issue three-weekly bulletins to a mailing list of about 3,500 people and publish a newsletter which is delivered locally to every building (10,000 doors!). We produce a 'corporate' brochure for Brindleyplace (now in its third edition) and, for each building, dedicated brochures and case study reports. Other activities include advertising, press briefings, opening events for both buildings and public spaces, seminars, lunches (and dinners) and participation in public events and conferences.

A footbridge over the Birmingham Canal leads from the International Convention Centre to the Water's Edge. Opposite: less than a year elapsed between the erection of the lift cores and the completion of Number Two.

Towards zero defects

John Rodaway

At Brindleyplace Tarmac Building has built four buildings for Argent and the procurement technique has developed progressively, *writes John Rodaway of Tarmac Building*. For the initial contract for Number One, Argent employed a concept architect and engineer for the structural and services design and obtained competitive bids from ourselves and Kyle Stewart for the detailed design and construction. Argent however did state that all future projects would be negotiated with either Kyle Stewart or ourselves, with Norwest Holst carrying out two specialist projects.

For Number Two Argent employed a concept architect and engineer but with a reduced brief, bringing in our design team at a much earlier stage. The project cost was obtained by means of 'true open book' negotiation, with an overriding marketplace value being agreed as a sort of guaranteed maximum price between us. We then set package targets to achieve the elemental cost plan that had been set with quantity surveyors Silk & Frazier. We developed the package targets with five key partners – frame, lifts, window cleaning, window and curtain walling and building services – all of which have a significant effect on design and hence costs.

For Number Four the procurement route was developed further, placing a greater reliance on the Tarmac team with Argent effectively only employing the concept architect. At the time of achieving planning consent, the contract value had been agreed and again the five key packages had been established by ourselves. While the design was being developed, a joint cost plan between Tarmac and Silk & Frazier was established as a rolling document, with key 'hold' points. Significant package fluctuations were experienced during the design period but by establishing a marketplace value at the outset and using package target principles we were able to concentrate on individual areas of concern.

For Number Six Argent involved us at the embryonic stage with the concept architect. No engineers were initially employed while spatial relationships were agreed by using in-house techniques. The structural and services engineers employed by Tarmac were brought in at a slightly later stage. The design underwent a significant evolutionary process during the early period and only when the basic form was understood did we involve the five key subcontractors. The project cost was again discussed and agreed with Argent to reflect a highly competitive marketplace value, although the final contract value is less than that agreed at the outset. Tarmac employed the full design team other than the concept architect and asked Silk & Frazier to produce our bill of quantities, to achieve greater inclusion and openness in the open book principle. During the development period we set up a series of workshops with potential suppliers to agree particular aspects of the design, for example, whether the frame was to be concrete or steel. When the project scope and cost was finally agreed, the contractors' proposals were submitted and we had achieved the most complete design so far, with the majority of the drawings being at construction issue. With Number Six Argent also incentivised us and our supply chain to achieve 'zero defects' at completion by agreeing a zero retention policy.

With all the projects the fundamentals of the cost plan are agreed at the outset. These include our profit level, the site establishment cost, preliminaries and design contingency and all fees for design, including fees paid to some of the designing specialists. The early involvement of builder and specialist subcontractors carries a cost and project management fees are therefore included. Even with this, however, the total fee cost on the latest building was below the market norm for this type of project.

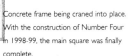

Concrete frame being craned into place. With the construction of Number Four in 1998-99, the main square was finally complete.

Teamwork in construction

Chris Gilmour

In August 1994 we received a telephone call from Argent, *writes Chris Gilmour of HBG Construction*. It was an invitation to design and build an office building, Number Five, that had been pre-let to BT and was to be delivered for a predetermined cost at a predetermined date. It marked the start of a working relationship that has to date involved over £100 million worth of projects.

Fundamental to developing a new process was the integration of both design and construction, early involvement of key subcontractors and suppliers and the establishment of a culture of trust and honesty, with trust being the key. For the system to work each team member was encouraged to make a significant contribution. Key specialist subcontractors were taken on board for the strength of their experience and the innovative approaches they had taken to their crafts. Their own expertise was exploited and incorporated into the design and specification of the building.

Just as Argent trusted HBG to complete the project successfully and were open and honest with the price, so HBG trusted its subcontractors and informed them how much each package was to be let for. Their opinions were always taken seriously and this trust was very important to the success of the project. From the client down, every member of the team was listened to and allowed to contribute.

Assembling the team at the beginning was key to the success of the project. The site manager was appointed along with planners, buyers and key subcontractors and suppliers before the outline design was complete. The next step was a full briefing of the entire team to ensure they all had a common understanding of what the project objectives were. Workshops were held to create a team culture.

Over a period of five months designs were developed, programmes tested and costs examined. At one point the cost plan reached £16.5 million yet with much hard work and innovation the project cost was reduced to £14.3 million, £200,000 less than the target. The savings were shared between HBG, the design team and the tenant.

Number Five was both started and completed on the days laid down in the schedule. The final account was agreed on the day of practical completion and HBG Construction and all its subcontractors profited. The quality of building was superb. It is a credit to everyone that worked on it and can be cited as a model for the construction industry.

It all sounds revolutionary. It is not. Pure common sense prevailed, simply bringing the right skills together at the right time – and providing us with a model we have now applied on all of our projects with Argent.

When construction of Number Five started in 1995, the landscaping of the main square, including the sculpture and footprint of the cafe, was already in place. Three years later construction of phase two, including Number Nine, was well under way.

Constructive framework

Ray Critchell

When we originally attended the steelwork subcontractor interviews for Brindleyplace, we were excited at the prospect of partnering, *writes Ray Critchell of Rowen Structures.* We little realised however the level of commitment that would be expected. Four years on and with almost 5,000 tonnes of steel fabricated, we feel we have overcome initial difficulties and realised the real benefits of partnering.

An essential aspect of the success of partnering at Brindleyplace was the early involvement of the specialist subcontractor in the conceptual design process. All too often this involvement begins too late, when there is limited scope for changes. But it is during this conceptual design stage that the specialist subcontractor can offer comments on material suitability, production preferences, buildability factors and commercial issues. These aspects can then be considered with a view to the simplification and rationalisation of the components, together with safety during erection. To achieve this requires close co-operation with the client's design team, the main contractor's design and site teams and other relevant subcontractors.

Transforming these ideas into practice has not been easy and each of the buildings we have been involved with – Numbers Two, Three, Five, Six and Nine – has offered particular challenges. The most demanding structure was Number Three, designed by Porphyrios Associates. This was due to both the exacting nature of the architectural requirements and the number of technical challenges that had to be overcome by the design team. Transfer structures at ground-floor level and composite steel/concrete columns were necessary to accommodate the basement car-parking layout. At sixth-floor level, a horizontal masonry movement joint was introduced, requiring a unique support system to carry the masonry/stonework above. At roof level, the structural support to the tower involved large transfer structures that had to be erected in sections onto a temporary support frame. In each case stringent deflection criteria were observed so as to avoid cracking to the masonry and stonework supported by the steel frame.

To compound these technical difficulties, a value engineering exercise had to run simultaneously to assess and control costs, together with discussions to ensure that the client's detailed requirements were met. But without a partnering arrangement in place, these difficulties would have been much greater and the costs proportionately higher.

Precast dentil being craned into position on the steel-framed clock tower of Number Three. Here modern construction is combined with an architectural vocabulary dating back to antiquity.

Component challenges

Alan Quartly

In securing the order for windows for the first office building at Brindleyplace, we embarked on an exciting new phase in the construction industry, *writes Alan Quartly of Glamalco*. Though our element of works was won in a competitive tender, Tarmac, the main contractor, was in partnership with the client. Number One proved to be a reasonable success for ourselves in performance while proving highly successful for Argent and Tarmac.

The next major development, Number Five, saw Glamalco appointed as subcontract partner to HBG Kyle Stewart. We secured the order after presenting a design brief and construction approach to both the main contractor and client. This was our first 'official' partnering charter. It enabled Glamalco to be involved in design of the curtain wall and windows plus associated products such as automatic blinds, cleaning access equipment, balustrading and smoke venting. It also allowed us to be involved with the building construction in general. This building was very successful for all parties in the partnering process, with the main contractor and architect being very receptive to our views. For this project the client initiated the use of video conferencing equipment for discussions between architect, contractor and ourselves, a very useful and efficient addition to our IT equipment.

Number Two followed a similar pattern, with Glamalco having a large involvement in the design process and gaining a greater understanding of the overall building construction. In our view, this was another successful contract with few problems during construction.

The window design process was pushed to the limits on Number Three. Despite a complicated building construction, in-depth discussion on window detailing involving the architect, Kawneer Systems and ourselves eventually achieved approval for the window design. Further complications on the design of the structure required sophisticated fixing principles to be designed in the bracketry. Again, a very successful conclusion with satisfaction for all departments involved.

Similarly Number Four offered new challenges, with a different architect and new design features for which solutions had to be found. Again with the assistance of Kawneer Systems, design detailing was achieved to meet the architect's design intent. Although the continuation of the design process during construction created new difficulties, continuous dialogue led to appropriate solutions. Partnering has continued in the design detailing for Numbers Nine, Six and Seven. Each project has seen total involvement from Glamalco from an early stage of design concept, estimating and manufacturing through to final installation.

In my view partnering can be achieved only when the client is committed to it and drives the project, calling for total involvement with all major trades. At Brindleyplace, Argent, Tarmac and HBG have allowed the specialist subcontractors to do what they do best – provide a service based on their own individual expertise.

Full-size mock-up of window, brickwork and stringcourse detail erected on the site of Number Five.

Lessons from Brindleyplace

Roger Madelin

1 Major regeneration can't work everywhere
Brindleyplace is strategically located on the main road between the established commercial core of central Birmingham and the important 'office suburb' of Edgbaston. Even so, the development could never have happened without the huge and well-judged investments (of largely EU money) made by the city in improving the local infrastructure and erecting landmark public buildings.

2 Large schemes need large sites
Birmingham city council assembled the 40 acre (16.2 hectare) site for the public buildings and the 17 acre (6.9 hectare) site for Brindleyplace by compulsory purchase. It is exceptionally difficult for private developers to assemble large sites at realistic prices and in recent years local authorities have become reluctant to use compulsory purchase powers. As Prince Charles observed, we have changed from Nimbys (Not In My Back Yard) to Bananas (Building Absolutely Nothing at All Near Anybody)! For large schemes to happen, there needs to be a vision for the project strong enough to counter adverse publicity and hostile pressure-groups. There also needs to be a strategy to bring sensible local people and pressure groups into the project. Above all, there needs to be capable and effective leadership from the local authority, supported by well-briefed officers and councillors.

3 A scheme must be sensible
At Brindleyplace the original would-be developer won the site by paying a large amount of money for a scheme that seemed optimistic even in the late 80s boom. Where sites are tendered by public bodies, they should not necessarily take the highest bid nor the most attractive sounding scheme: they should consider as far as possible what can work and who can make it work. Likewise the developer must not overpay. Far too often, developers pay too much for the site and then do everything in a rush and cut corners. The result is bad development.

4 Delays must be kept to a minimum
Argent would not have purchased the site if we had not been able to get going quickly. We were able to do so because, during the receivership of the previous developer, a new consent had been granted for a different mix of uses. The masterplan that accompanied that consent was unsuitable for our purposes but our revised masterplan, which kept the permitted mix of uses but re-arranged them on the site, was approved swiftly by the planners.

5 The market cannot be ignored
Brindleyplace has cost hundreds of millions of pounds to develop. To raise that kind of money, the commercial elements must satisfy the requirements of large occupiers and financial institutions while the residential elements must satisfy the requirements of owners and mortgage lenders. A broad mix of uses within a single building (as distinct from a similar mix in different buildings within an overall scheme) is, for a whole range of reasons, very difficult to fund in the UK, although there are some signs that this is beginning to change.

6 Design must be co-ordinated
We wanted different architects to design particular buildings but to work within our overall brief in terms of materials, colonnades, cornice lines etc. The architects were carefully selected so that they would work closely with us and with each other. Where we sold parts of the site, for example for the housing and Sealife Centre, we tried (not always as successfully as we would have liked) to retain as much control as we could over design and timing.

7 Landscape before buildings
Too often, landscape is an afterthought. For Brindleyplace we held a landscape design competition at the outset and the landscape architect we appointed has worked closely with the architects of all the buildings. Similarly, the question of how people, cars and service vehicles will move around the scheme has to be carefully addressed at the master-planning stage. Care must be given to views (both short and long) from every part of the scheme. A good mixed-use town centre scheme has to pay attention to its context, knitting together jagged edges, forming part of the urban fabric and creating continuity and order.

8 Be wary if residential development comes first
My home is my castle! The residents of the houses at Brindleyplace delayed one phase of the project by

at least a year, costing us at least a million pounds. The cost was probably much more, since office tenants were lost because buildings were not available when they ought to have been.

9 Be realistic with residential
It might have been better if the residential component of Brindleyplace had been of higher density and more closely integrated with the rest of the scheme. But we had to provide what the market wanted – security, privacy and parking. The three acre (1.2 hectare) triangular site has the canal on two sides and a secure front on the third. Only when it is demonstrably safe from crime and traffic will urban housing (particularly housing for a mix of people) be more integrated into the city.

10 Pay more for planning
Despite having a very 'detailed' outline planning consent with an agreed masterplan, which included building massing, we have still been required to submit detailed applications for each individual building, under a reserved matters application. Some applications have been treated by the planning committee as 'fair game'. Council officers are professional and helpful but they are overworked and under-resourced. We believe that developers pay far too little for submitting a planning application. We would be happy to pay more in return for a more timely service.

11 Allow flexible consents for buildings
Why not have a flexible building consent, permitting use of the building as office, college, shops, restaurants or residential? We had a proposal for a College of Law at Brindleyplace, which might have been financed if the city had authorised possible subsequent use of the buildings as offices. Instead they said it would have to be used as a college but if in the future the college left, there might be a possibility that other uses could be considered. On this basis, funding was not possible.

12 There's nothing wrong with tall buildings
The debate on the height of buildings should be re-opened. In New York, you find 60-storey buildings next to 150-year old brownstone houses but in the UK a proposal to build two or three storeys

above an adjacent building can cause a riot in the planning committee. The key questions are: how does it look and what will it contribute to the long-term vitality and prosperity of the city?

13 People have to get to work
Car parking is still a major factor when companies choose an office location. Denying parking spaces without providing or facilitating attractive, alternative means of transport is unrealistic. It is not acceptable to occupiers or funders and may well mean that an otherwise worthwhile development will not happen at all. Until public transport is improved, we have to design for the car – which is not to say that design has to be dictated by the car.

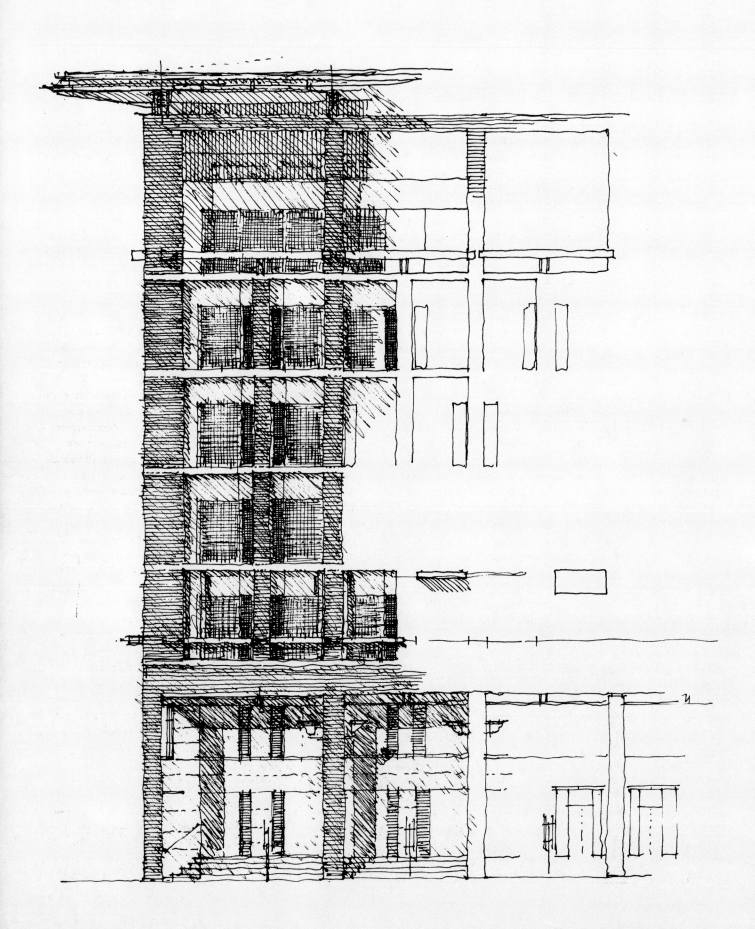

Chapter five: Buildings and squares

David Partridge

The masterplan of Brindleyplace is essentially about spaces with buildings around them. Once we had reviewed the disposition of uses and spaces, the first thing to do when Argent bought the site was to choose the designer of the urban spaces. The detailed design of the Water's Edge had already been largely completed by Benoy and we quickly made the decision to press on with it, with only minimal amendments.

We tried to find out who had designed any brand-new city squares in the UK in the previous ten years. We found that the only ones were Broadgate, initially designed by Peter Foggo – who tragically had since died – and Canary Wharf, which we felt was too North American. We spoke to the Landscape Institute and received a list, from which we chose ten names and asked for examples of their work. We met about five and made a shortlist of two, to which we later added Robert Townshend, and asked them to produce a scheme in a limited competition.

The brief was to carry out a two- to three-week design exercise for the central square. Urban design guidelines were produced by John Chatwin, setting out the main constraints on the space from traffic, pedestrians, servicing, ground levels and the uses which would surround the square. The difficult part of the brief was that the square was going to be built first, before any buildings, and so would need to be of a strong enough design to stand on its own; yet ultimately it would become a space between buildings and so should not compete with them.

One of the proposals was for a cool, understated

space, somewhat lacking in character, while the second was perhaps too dominant, like a stage without a play. But Robert Townshend's scheme was perfect. It struck exactly the right balance between interest when empty of people (or buildings) and activity when full. The use of water and the curving steps and grass implied an amphitheatre where planned events could take place but which would still seem natural on a cold February afternoon with few people about. It also offered opportunities for a fountain, sculpture and a central feature such as a cafe. Without hesitation we asked Townshends to start working up the scheme.

We also conducted a small competition for the sculptural events envisaged in the Townshend landscape plan. We interviewed a number of public art organisations and then, having chosen the Royal Society of British Sculptors, ran through a long and short list of potential artists. We wanted a piece which would capture the 'genius' of Brindleyplace – water, iron, industrial – as well as a piece which would both respond to and interact with its specific setting. Having whittled the list down to three, we chose Miles Davies who had produced a series of pieces in black metal (actually patinated phosphor bronze) with canal-like themes – lock gates, aqueducts and bridges. With a grant from the Association for the Business Sponsorship of the Arts, we proceeded with one piece at the entrance to Brindleyplace and another in the main square.

Before we actually started construction of the square and the main spine road, however, we wanted to test the robustness of the design by putting some buildings around it. We also needed some images with buildings to market our vision. Fortunately, there had been a lot more office buildings constructed in the previous ten years than new urban spaces. Unfortunately in our view not many of them were very good and we were particularly determined to avoid the postmodern excesses of the late 80s.

We wanted to find architects who fitted some fairly exacting criteria. In the first place, we wanted to work with practices of a size that would guarantee us direct involvement from the principals themselves. We felt that the top rank of the medium-sized, well-regarded, up-and-coming designers would be hungrier than the big firms and would

Opposite: early elevational study for Number Six by Allies & Morrison. Below: Preliminary proposal for the main square by Townshends.

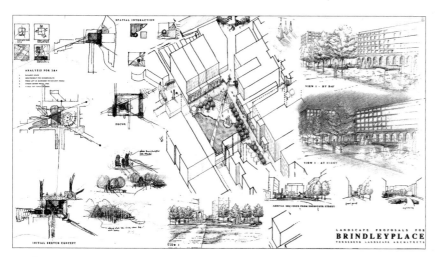

listen to us. We wanted these buildings to be one of the most important commissions for the practice. We did not want either a superstar – who we might only meet in person on a couple of occasions but who would influence the process from afar – nor one of the large commercial practices who churned out offices by the square foot. We wanted not just to be listened to as a client but also to engage in a debate directly with the people who were making the design decisions. We wanted to make sure that our view was understood first-hand and we wanted to understand the designer at first-hand too.

We also wanted architects who were used to building in brick. We felt that Birmingham was intrinsically a brick city and that brick would fit more naturally into the urban scale that we were trying to create than the panellised systems in vogue at the time (Stockley Park, Canary Wharf, Broadgate etc). We also felt that brick was more acceptable institutionally and, most important of all, it was cheaper. The sorts of rents we were going to achieve were £15 to £20 per square foot – the last time we had had to build down to this level was in a 30,000 square foot (2,790 square metre) building in Luton in 1987. It was going to be tough to design to this budget and achieve the internal quality and external gravitas required. And from this stemmed our last criterion – that the architects would have to be flexible enough to work closely with the construction team and other consultants to achieve a tight cost plan.

Once we had crossed out anyone who didn't meet our criteria, there were not many names left! We asked for brochures from about 15, interviewed about ten and got down to a short list of four: Edward Cullinan; Anthony Peake (who used to be at Cullinan's – both of whom we had worked with before); and Sidell Gibson and Demetri Porphyrios, who were part of the Paternoster team.

We gave each architect a building facing the square and asked them to work up a scheme design. John Chatwin set out the urban design guidelines for each plot and we worked individually with each designer to achieve efficient office floor-plates, with plenty of natural light. Chatwin also co-ordinated a set of indicative rules relating to arcades and attic storeys but these were not prescriptive in terms of dimensions or levels.

For the first two weeks the architects worked in

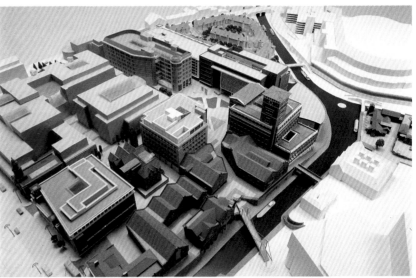

isolation, co-ordinated by John Chatwin and ourselves. Then we brought them together around a 1:200 cardboard model of the square prepared by Townshends. We met at the offices of our engineers Ove Arup & Partners and each architect ceremonially put his own model into place. In the meantime, following his wonderfully successful public toilet/flower stall in Westbourne Grove, we had appointed Piers Gough of CZWG to design a 'gem' in the form of a cafe for the centre of the square. He produced his model with a flourish from a matchbox.

And then we stood back. Demetri Porphyrios' building, Number Three, was clearly at the ceremonial head of the square, fully frontalised and symmetrical but with an off-centre tower 'belonging to Birmingham and not Brindleyplace', embedded in the urban block with the Water's Edge but acting as a long-distance marker. Paul Gibson's Number Five stood opposite, with a long, cavernous atrium pulling light deep into the plan but pared back by the diagonal cut of the main entrance avenue to expose its entrance. The situation with Numbers Two (Ted Cullinan) and Four (Tony Peake) was not as clear-cut, so they were put on hold, but even so we had enough to get going on the construction of the square.

The market then took over fully. British Telecom wanted 120,000 square feet (11,160 square metres) and we quickly enlarged Paul Gibson's Number Five to fit their requirements. The narrow clear-span floor plates and openness across the atrium also ideally suited BT's Workstyle 2000 new working practices. We had also agreed with a fund to commence construction of Number One and appointed Tony Peake. A scheme had previously been submitted for planning permission, so we had to rework the plan within an agreed urban design framework to replace the central core with our inner atrium. Construction started straight away.

In the meantime, our initial reassessment of the masterplan had relocated the housing to the triangle site and it was well underway with a scheme by Max Lyons of Lyons Sleeman Hoare. The Sealife Centre was chasing the leisure site and we suggested that, if there was going to be a blank box, it had better be by someone like Norman Foster!

One of our head-lease obligations was to refurbish the exterior of Martin & Chamberlain's grade 2 listed Oozells Street School and by this stage this too was well underway. We were approached by the Ikon Gallery, who were looking to relocate from their existing premises and had developed a scheme with Axel Burrough of Levitt Bernstein for remodelling the interior and adding new liftshafts for people and artworks.

We were then approached by Lloyds Bank, who were looking to relocate their regional offices. They wanted 75,000 square feet (6,975 square metres) and the only building which fitted this was Number Two. We had already opened discussions with Allies & Morrison, who had been a close runner-up in our initial shortlist. Lloyds' in-house architectural team were keen to work with them, so we quickly forged a scheme with the floor-plates arranged around an atrium. An eroded corner with the satellite core took in the diagonal axis leading from the International Convention Centre, over the new bridge, through the Water's Edge and into the square. It also had a double-height colonnade facing the square and a set-back to the upper floor. The elevations, a play on different planes of brick and metalwork, were recessive, acting as a cool backdrop to the drama of Porphyrios' Number Three.

The design of Number Three also proceeded apace, with a view to a speculative start on site in early 1996. Attention then began to focus on Number Four, to fill in the large gap between the multi-storey car park and health club (won in a limited competition by Benoy and Norwest Holst) and Number Three. We were not happy with the previous elevations and decided to instigate a small design competition. Again we interviewed about half-a-dozen practices, all of whom met our original criteria, and made a shortlist of Stanton Williams, Lifschutz Davidson, Jeremy Dixon/Edward Jones and Anthony Peake.

Stanton Williams was by far the boldest but this unashamedly modernist scheme was a perfect link between Five and Three. One end related to the tower of Number Five and the entrance axes along Oozells Street and across the square from the Water's Edge, while the other provided a mass similar to Number Two, to frame Number Three. There was a tall deep colonnade under this, with the opportunity for a fantastic restaurant to spill out into it and over the canal on the other side. We had

Phase two of Brindleyplace addresses the area between Broad Street and the main square. From top: Number Six (Allies & Morrison), Numbers Eight and Ten (Sidell Gibson) and Number Seven (Porphyrios Associates).
Opposite: views of early model showing Water's Edge (Benoy), Number One (Anthony Peake Associates), Number Three (Porphyrios Associates), Number Four (Anthony Peake Associates), Number Two (Allies & Morrison) and Number Five (Sidell Gibson); later model with new design for Number Four by Stanton Williams.

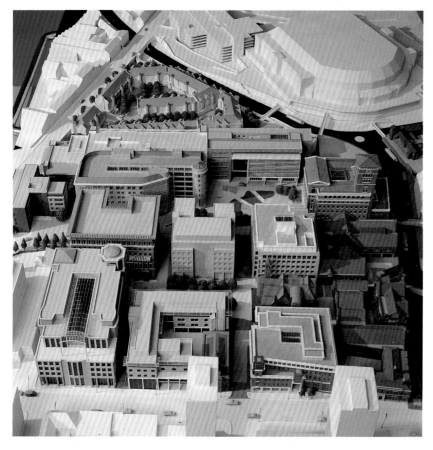

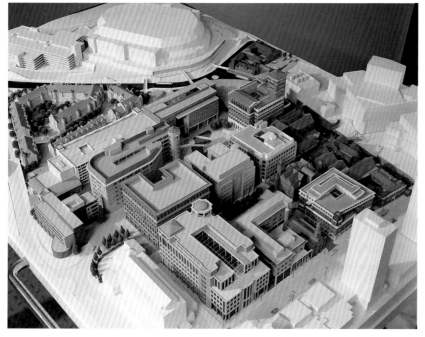

Above and opposite: 1999 model and plan of Brindleyplace.

some reservations as to whether or not Birmingham was ready for this, but decided to press ahead. Some 18 months later, and after much chopping-away of the canalside elevation, we achieved planning consent. The problem was the residents of the housing on the other side of the canal, some of whom complained that they hadn't realised that there was going to be any development opposite them! The modern design was also a stumbling block.

Our attention now turned to phase two and the creation of a new square to complement the first one, which by now sported the award-winning all-glass cafe by Piers Gough. We invited Bob Allies, Graham Morrison and Demetri Porphyrios to a number of sessions with John Chatwin to agree on the urban design basis for the new square. We wanted something which provided a suitable setting for the Ikon Gallery but also gave flexibility for the remaining plots. There was also the problem of finding a sensible plan for the building on the south side of the square, Number Nine, which would have to relate to the listed church on Broad Street. We came up with the idea of a long narrow space focusing on the Ikon at one end and a feature building (ie Number Eight) at the other. Flanking it would be Number Six, which fronted both squares, and Number Nine, which wrapped around the church to form a single urban block with a central open courtyard.

We asked Robert Townshend to develop the scheme for Oozells Square to act as a counter balance to the main square. Working closely with stone sculptor Paul de Monchaux, he came up with a cooler, almost Zen-like, space defined by cherry trees and linked from end to end by a glass-like water feature. In contrast to the architecturally busy central square, it will have more direct activity, with the art gallery, offices and restaurants spilling out onto it from the adjacent buildings.

We chose Associated Architects for Number Nine because we wanted to use a Birmingham firm and its recent work in the Jewellery Quarter was highly praised. We then chose Demetri Porphyrios and Paul Gibson for Numbers Seven and Eight (the latter eventually became two buildings) because we were so pleased with their work. Porphyrios got Number Seven because it meant that there would be an interesting continuity between the first office

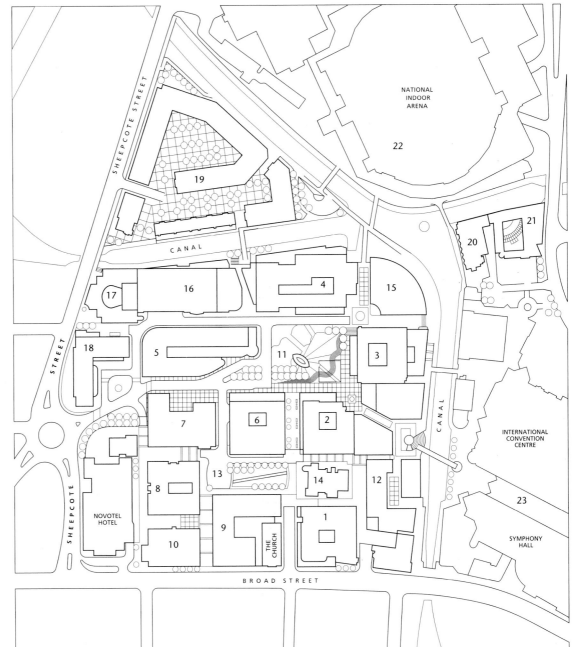

building you meet as you drive in and the last, standing at the head of the square. This implied line of tension also provided the key to the plan of the building, U-shaped but with a shorter leg to allow the central square to expand into the entrance courtyard and be terminated by the longer leg. It meant that Number Seven was a building belonging to the square, not the entrance.

We then chose Allies & Morrison for Number Six, the building between the two squares. Number Two was regarded by some as a bit bland and we didn't want the same thing right next door. So we asked Bob Allies and Graham Morrison, in a competition of one, to come up with a building which was the same but different! – which they did.

The key to the evolution of the design has been maintaining a subtle balance both between spaces and buildings and between the buildings themselves. Every element has been designed in its place and for its place. Each element has had to react in an evolutionary fashion both to the built form existing at the time of its inception and to the putative vision for its neighbours which might follow. By combining this approach with a variety of different uses, each feeding off the other, we hope that Brindleyplace will feel like a piece of real city – intrinsically and seamlessly linked into its surroundings rather than an office ghetto which might have sprung up overnight and been grafted on to the urban continuum like some alien form.

Townshend Landscape

Brindleyplace Square

In 1994 Argent invited Townshend Landscape Architects to enter a competition to design the main square at their newly acquired site at Brindleyplace, *writes Robert Townshend*. The competition brief, which included the initial urban design guidelines prepared by John Chatwin, called for the square to:

• act as a natural extension to the sequence of public spaces running through the centre of Birmingham.

• be of sufficient stature to create an 'address' at the heart of the development while also addressing the buildings that were going to border it.

• be an integral part of the network of public spaces that would link all parts of Brindleyplace, but which at that time were loosely defined.

• accommodate all the necessary service and servicing routes associated with a development of this size.

• be sufficiently robust to respond to change over time, and yet retain its character.

• be capable of being built within the prescribed budget and development programme.

To this we added an aspiration to create a dynamic space, imbued with a spirit of optimism at a time when the economy was beginning to show signs of recovery.

Analysis of the early masterplan established an understanding of the anticipated vistas, circulation routes, micro-climatic conditions and changes in level. From this we established the need for a principle point of focus at the heart of the space – the Piers Gough cafe – which would terminate the views into the site from the International Convention Centre, Broad Street and Sheepcote Street and provide a hub of activity and movement. Secondary

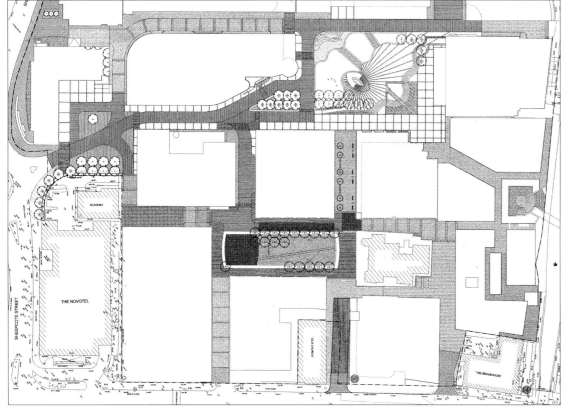

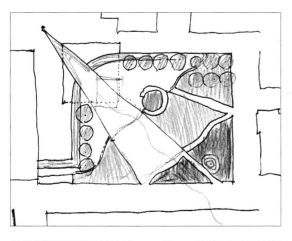

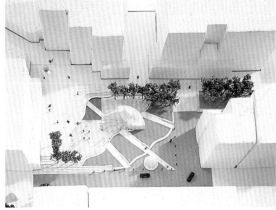

points were identified at the ends of the east-west diagonal axis across the square, which would strengthen the pedestrian links with the ICC and terminate one of the principal views across the square. These became the water feature to the east, where the moving water captures and reflects the light throughout the day, and the Miles Davies sculpture to the west, which acts as a reminder of the historic past of Brindleyplace. By utilising the change in level across the square we could create an amphitheatre in the centre of it adjacent to the cafe, in the warmest and sunniest spot.

The change in level of approximately one metre from east to west across the square allowed the introduction of a series of strata, each indicating a different use. At the upper level to the east, the simply patterned York stone paving addresses the fronts of Buildings Two and Three, and also accommodates the fire route and other emergency services needs. The sinuous limestone steps double up as seats, as well as a cascade, and cast varying shadows under the changing conditions. The starburst pattern, made up of only two differently dimensioned pieces of York stone, radiates from the cafe, emphasising the active use of the space as well as reinforcing the focus on the building, while

the tilting grass planes contain and shield it from the road on the west side and provide a pool of colour throughout the year. Finally, the trees – Liquidambar styraciflua on the south side and Gingko biloba on the north – anchor the corners of the square.

At night the square takes on a different character. The fountains become candles; lit from beneath, they entrap the light as they rise and fall in endless variations. The cafe sheds glowing light through its transparent structure, while the sculpture and trees are more softly uplit to mark the extremities of the space.

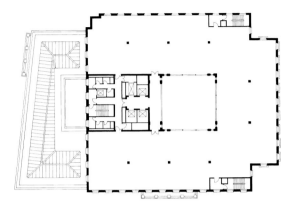

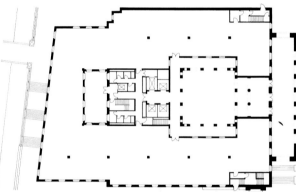

Porphyrios
Associates

Number Three

Three Brindleyplace occupies a key position at the head of the main square. It provides 91,500 square feet (8,500 square metres) of office space on six floors plus a 50 metre high tower that provides a landmark for Brindleyplace.

The massing of Number Three is additive, *writes Porphyrios Associates*. The building presents a civic front to the square and steps down to three storeys towards the Birmingham canal. The tower rises as if embedded within the urban block and serves as a landmark for the entire Brindleyplace development. The main entrance leads through a double-height arcade into a lofty foyer, which in turn opens onto the central seven-storey glazed atrium.

The atrium is the heart of the building, revealing at once its organisation in plan and section. It has an ashlar stone base with an arcade at ground floor; a columniated middle; and a loggia at the top surmounted by the glazed roof. The aim is to project a light post-and-spandrel structure in contrast to the solidity of the external masonry, thereby revealing the twin constructional principles of loadbearing wall masonry and steel frame.

At each office level, lifts open onto broad balconies overlooking the atrium. The 13 metre floor plate and 2.7 metre floor-to-ceiling height provide good working conditions with ample natural light and the potential for natural ventilation.

The external walls of the steel-framed building are of self-supporting brick and ashlar stone construction. All architectural projections and rusticated surfaces are in reconstituted stone. Windows are detailed in metal and roofs are in terne-coated steel sheeting. Cornices, window-surrounds and string courses lend the building a sculptural character and ornamental profiles underline its constructional reading, while motifs like anthemia, reeds, roundels and acroteria are used for punctuation or to soften

Unlike most other modem large buildings the envelope of Three Brindleyplace carries its own weight directly to the foundations, *writes Richard Henley of Ove Arup & Partners*. By separating the outer wall leaf from the structural frame the usual consequences of accommodating the marriage of a stiff wall and a relatively flexible frame are eliminated. By thoughtful consideration of movements, horizontal restraint details, mortar design and the influences of the construction process, the natural brick coursing is broken only to form movement joints at the corners of the main building.

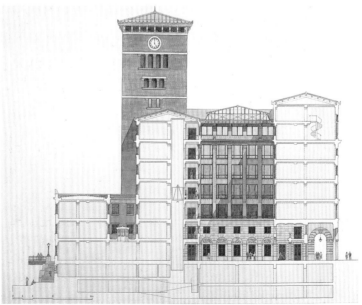

the skyline.

On the elevation to the main square, the interweaving of the arcade arches gives a pictorial depth to the plane of the wall, with half-round relieving arches transferring the weight onto piers and quarter-engaged Doric columns. Thus a figure-ground dialogue emerges: from a structural viewpoint the half-round arch is the figure, while the pointed arch becomes a figure only on account of the resultant void. This oscillation in the reading is heightened by the memory of the trabeated system to which the Doric columns allude. Here, where the building addresses the public square, the history of western structural traditions is narrated in stone.

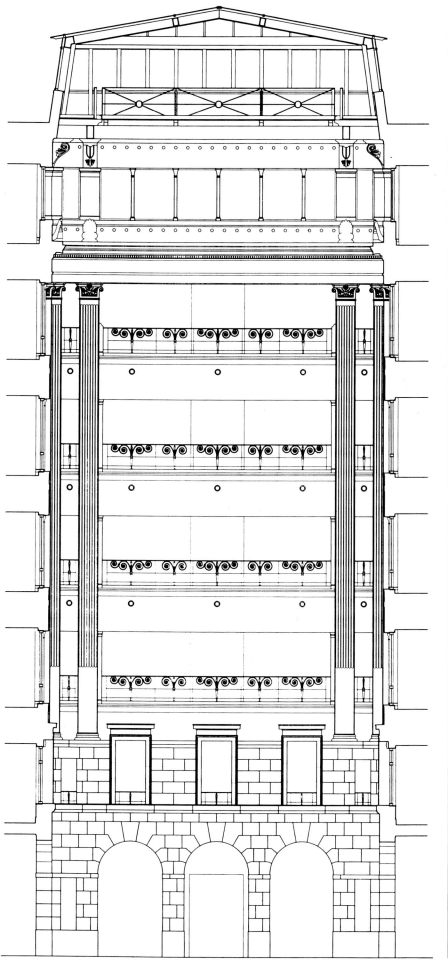

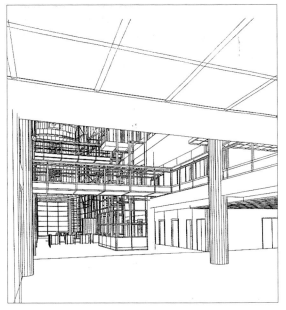

Sidell Gibson

Number Five

Number Five stands at the west end of the main square, with a 35 metre frontage overlooking the square and a depth of some 85 metres.

The design of the building started from its position in relation to the square, *writes Sidell Gibson Partnership*. This allowed a clear understanding of the sense of the place, the arrival points and the best views. Good views out for the people working inside the building are provided by the long atrium with its large glass wall at the end, seven floors high, giving panoramic views of the square. At night time especially the opposite is also true and one is able to see right into the heart of the

building from across the main square.

When BT decided to occupy the building, they wanted the interior to have a focal point where staff would meet naturally. With them we developed the idea of visible circulation, with glass lifts, a prominent spiral stair near the entrance and dramatic bridges across the atrium.

From the outset Number Five was conceived as a low-energy building. Ventilation is by upflow air-conditioning via 400mm deep floor voids, and windows are kept as small as practical, commensurate with good daylighting. Budget constraints were also very significant, in that Birmingham

rental values are about half those in London, so a highly cost-effective design was imperative.

The architectural challenge was to reconcile these various ideas and requirements. The solution was a form in brick and reconstructed stone that is like a castle, with towers marking the entrance. A sense of drama is created, with the curved forms providing perspectives and views that change as you approach the building. On entry there is the additional surprise of seeing the atrium extending into the depth of the building and ending in stepped balconies, which are planted to resemble a green valley.

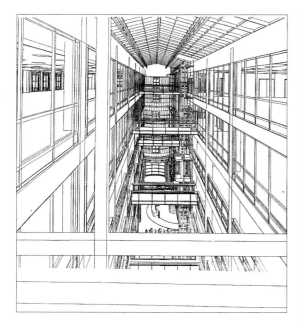

In visual terms the atrium reduces the apparent bulk of the building when seen from the main square and continues the public realm of the square into the heart of the 85 metre deep building. A preliminary elevation study is shown below.

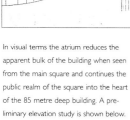

ENTRANCE ELEVATION

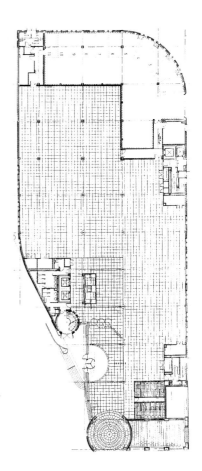

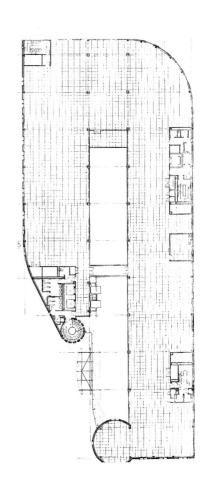

The visible circulation – glass lifts, bridges and spiral stair – animate the atrium and make it the social heart of the building. The ground-floor cafe bar and 'oasis' areas provided on each floor create opportunities for informal meeting and socialising for the 1,200 BT staff working in the building.

In moving to the new offices, BT wanted to replace the rigidity of a cellular layout with the flexibility and variety provided by open-plan. Number Five has played a formative role in 'Workstyle 2000', BT's company-wide drive to increase efficiency through flexible, varied and collaborative ways of working.

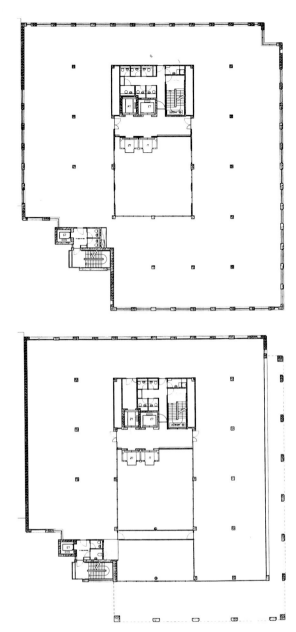

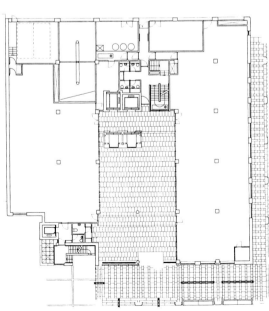

Allies & Morrison

Number Two

Number Two provides 75,000 square feet (6,975 square metres) of office space on seven floors around a central full-height atrium. The building is determined both by its own internal organisation and by its response to the context of the overall masterplan, *writes Allies & Morrison.*

While the 13.5 metre deep office space provides a simple repeated discipline to the building's interior, the outside is affected by its location and orientation, the hierarchy within the masterplan and the diagonal cut of the route from the Water's Edge. The plan, organised axially, gives a logical sequence from the landscaped square through a six

metre high colonnade (continuous with neighbouring buildings), double-height entrance, 30 metre high atrium and freestanding lift tower, giving access to each office floor. Two lifts with glass backs rise in a perforated metal screen which, with its backlighting, illuminates and animates the atrium. Two further lifts, along with toilet accommodation and the principal stair, are contained in the core. A second core with a fully glazed stair is located on the corner facing the water's edge, marking the diagonal cut of the approach to the main square. The colonnade, on the principal facade overlooking the main square, forms the base of

The diagonal route from the city centre
is incised into the set-back corner of the
building, which at night becomes the
backdrop for the 'civic theatre' created
by the fountains and cafe in the square.

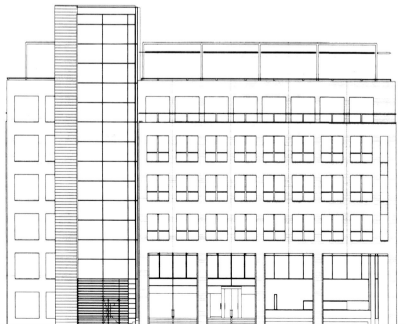

the tripartite composition, with the middle formed by the office grid and the top by the recessed pavilion floor.

Each of the facades is layered in detail to effect a particular response to orientation and context. The front is formal and deliberate; the side facing Oozells Street is asymmetrical and inflected towards the main square; and the back is simple and robust, providing the entrance to the two levels of basement car parking and the enclosed service yards. The facades are constructed of loadbearing brick on a steel frame. Fenestration in silver-grey painted metalwork forms a continuous lattice as a counterpoint to the masonry and a

link to the white-plastered interior. The colonnade and recessed upper storey are rendered to give the interior character of an inner layer.

The street-level colonnade tempers the division between public and private and brings the life of the square within the perimeter of the building.

Stanton Williams

Number Four

A city is defined by its public spaces, *writes Stanton Williams*. The urban plan for Brindleyplace recognises this fact – buildings are not merely isolated objects, each on their own plot of land. Growing a piece of city opens up important creative possibilities that go beyond mere right-of-light envelopes, flow patterns and planning guidelines.

Brindleyplace explores these possibilities, building upon the traditional vocabulary of city space types. The architecture of the buildings forms the spaces in-between and orchestrates the way that they are used and seen. Buildings and urban space are thus locked together in close relationship.

Our approach to the design of Number Four derives from this. The last and largest building on the main square, it both responds to and defines the spaces around it. Our competition-winning design established the basic concept. The building form is determined on the one hand by the need to achieve an appropriate sense of scale and enclosure for the square and the continuity of the building facades around it; and on the other by the need to break down the scale to respond to the residential development on the canal side. The higher volume established for the square, aligning with the cornice lines of its neighbours, is

Number Four Brindleyplace is a seven-storey building with 112,000 square feet (10,415 square metres) of office space on the upper floors, providing extensive views. The large open office floor plates (20,000 square feet/1,860 square metres) are designed for flexible, multi-tenant occupation, with a choice of energy and environmental control systems including part natural ventilation. The spaces are organised around three service cores and a 40 metre long by 30 metre high glazed atrium that draws light into the heart of the building. Also included on the ground floor is a 10,000 square foot (930 square metre) restaurant that extends out under the colonnade on the main square and links through to a canal side terrace at the rear. There is also a two-storey basement car park.

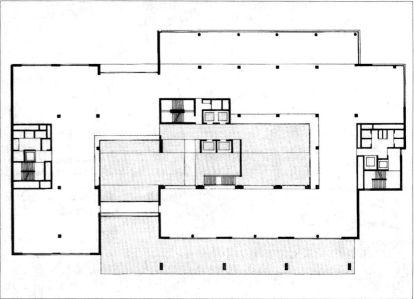

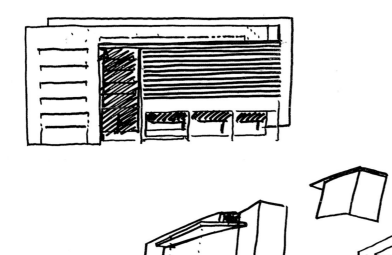

maintained at the north-east end to balance the height of Number Three. Both buildings act as a gateway to the square when seen from across the canal and also as a backdrop to the curved form of the National Sealife Centre.

The facade to the square has four major elements. The space of the square is extended into the building by the tall main entrance, located at the point where the pedestrian axis and view from the International Convention Centre meets the axis along Oozells Street from Broad Street. The colonnade maintains the full height of the other colonnades on adjacent buildings and, as the square

The composition of the main elevation facing the square responds to the main elements of the masterplan, including the diagonal route across the square and the access into the square from Broad Street via Oozells Street. Behind the colonnade is a large restaurant enjoying views over the main square.

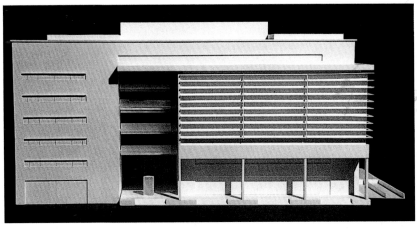

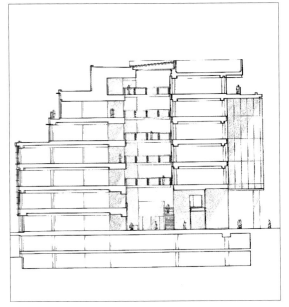

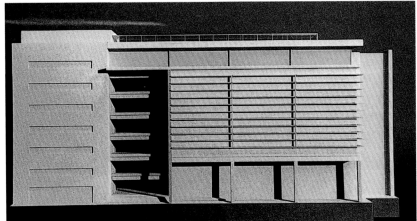

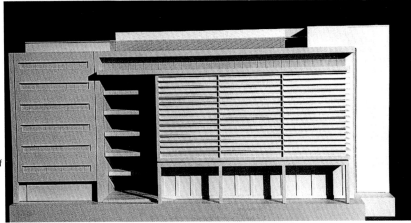

slopes down towards the building, thereby holds the space of the square. The louvred screen facade in metal and glass responds to the elevation of Number Two opposite and completes the view towards Number Three at the head of the square. A tall solid element in brick, making a visual link to Number Five, terminates the building against the multi-storey car park and establishes the corner of the square.

To the north east, the building is planned around the sub-square that leads to the entrance to the National Sealife Centre. Stepped, vertical elements join the facade on the square to the more

terraced forms of the canal side of the building. Where the building faces the canal and residential development, it steps down and articulates itself into a series of volumes responding in scale, materials and fenestration. The main volume, perceived as six storeys from the canal, is faced in brick, while a lower volume that is more transparent in detail relates in height to the Sealife Centre. A landscaped terrace base containing plant and parking aligns with the canal tow path and the adjacent health club.

The building is constructed as a concrete frame with solid elements of Belgian brick, flush-pointed to give a feeling of mass and continuity of   surface. Metal panels and detailing give

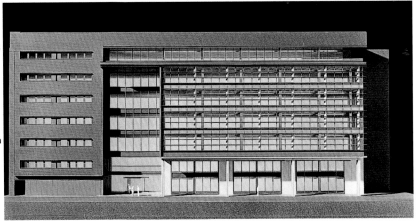

71

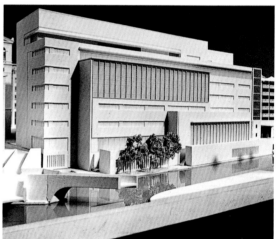

the building an appropriate scale. Transparent elements draw light and space through the volumes. A precast concrete base forms the colonnade and, together with the brick volume, folds into the entrance and atrium space, thus giving continuity between inside and out.

The brick end wall of the atrium establishes continuity between the main exterior and interior public spaces. On the canal side, the massing of the building is broken down into a number of different elements, in part to meet objections from residents of the Symphony Court housing on the other side of the canal.

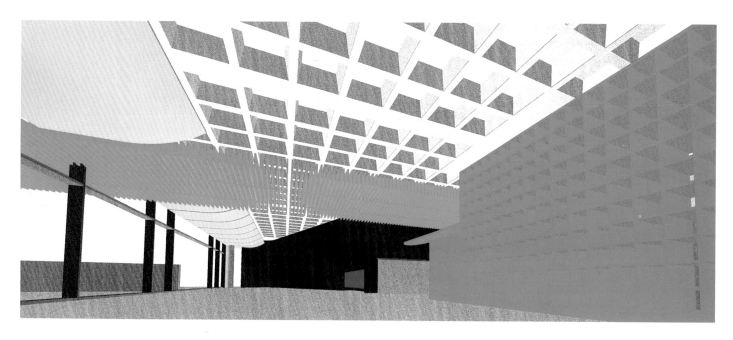

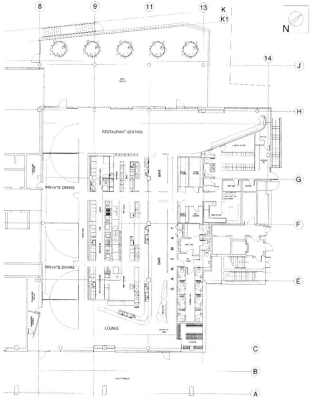

Wickham & Associates

Restaurant

The Bank restaurant occupies the eastern end of the ground floor of Number Four, *writes Wickham & Associates*. It provides 150 covers in the main restaurant plus a further 100 covers in private dining areas. These are enclosed with large pivoting glass partitions which may be opened to increase the size of the main restaurant or vary the capacity of the private dining areas. The bar takes 50 covers. The kitchen, situated in the centre of the plan, will be open, allowing views through the entire length of the restaurant, from the main square to the canal. The terrace at the rear allows diners to enjoy the canal.

Piers Gough
CZWG

Cafe

The cafe was designed as the centrepiece of the main square and the focal point for the Brindleyplace development, *writes CZWG Architects*. Only 14 metres long and a maximum of 7.6 metres wide, the eye-shaped glass-and-steel structure seats 40 people inside, with provision for over 100 covers alfresco. The square also contains sculptures, a water feature and 'sculpted' grass areas and the building continues this sculptural theme.

Structural columns, which are continuous with roof members, intersect at the ridge to form canopies which mirror the footprint of the building and increase its vertical presence in the square. The tubular steel frame supports 143 separate pieces of glass in 32 different shapes. Glazing consists mainly of double-glazed units with a white dot-fritted outer pane. The canopy has the same frit but is single-glazed, helping protection against glare and solar gain. The fritting continues to a transom line above the door head. Below this, the glazing is either clear toughened (looking onto the cafe areas) or solid white fritted (in front of insulated partitions to the kitchen and wc's). Specially extruded aluminium sections secure the glazing, incorporating weather seals around the plate glass doors.

To ensure that the glass was cut correctly, the steel structure was erected at the factory for glazing templates to be made, before being dismantled and re-erected on site.

The base of the cafe sits over the centre of a radiating pattern of York stone which visually links the interior and exterior. Secure storage and pumping space is provided at basement level, hidden from view to maintain the transparency of the cafe. Prominent within the space are a curved zinc-topped bar with metallic fascia, flush glass chiller unit and zinc back bar with glass shelving. Glass shelves holding bottles are lit from below by concealed light fittings. Low voltage pendant luminaires with adjustable conical shades are suspended from the soffit of the perimeter duct and can be directed over the tables. Secondary uplighters are located on top of the duct to flood-light the roof space, lighting the casket of the cafe at night and silhouetting the signage.

Summer cooling is aided by the main fold-back glass doors, with external air pumped in overhead. Heated air pumped in for winter warming is supplemented by underfloor heating. The separate air supply and extract for the kitchen is provided by the sculpted stone vents in the adjoining grassed area plus a louvered funnel duct.

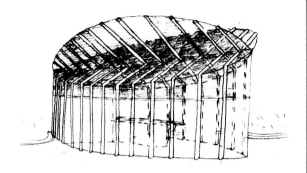

Cafe Bruu

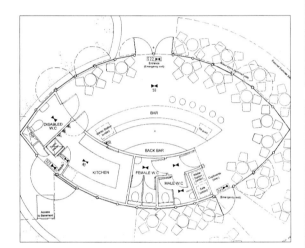

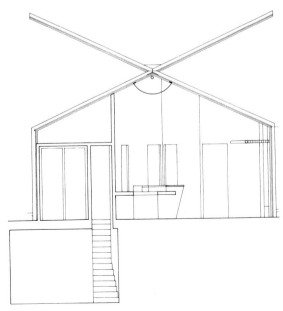

Located on the corner of the Birmingham and Brindley Loop canals, the National Sealife Centre forms part of the series of leisure attractions, including the National Indoor Arena and International Convention Centre (with Symphony Hall), bringing visitors from around the UK to this part of the city.

Foster & Partners

Sealife Centre

The National Sealife Centre is the biggest collection of both native freshwater and marine creatures in Europe, including sharks, sting rays and eels. It occupies a prominent waterside location at the north-east corner of Brindleyplace at the junction of the Birmingham canal system.

The shape of the building is derived from the marine exhibits themselves, *writes Foster & Partners*, with the sweeping structure modelled on the profile of a ray. The gross external area of 43,350 square feet (4,030 square metres) and net internal area of 38,700 square feet (3,600 square metres) includes exhibition space, retail, catering and educational facilities plus the fit-out, designed by Vardon Attractions. A faceted solid wall facing the canal is expressed as an articulated plane by recessing the glass stairs at each end. The roof is articulated from the walls with a narrow glass slot and blue painted steelwork. A precast concrete base wraps around the building, providing a tough external surface which takes up the differing ground levels and gradients. The roof has a double curvature and is finished in a mid-grey polymeric material.

Two lifts convey visitors to the lower ground/canalside level. From here they enter the main tank, containing over 325,000 litres of water. A curving acrylic tunnel turns into a 360° transparent viewing tunnel, with water and marine life all around. A vertical tunnel at the exit of the display area allows another glimpse of the feature tank, while a further porthole on the external wall to the canal offer glimpses into the tank from outside. Glass slots in the stairs and glazing in the temporary exhibition and cafe area further animate the building.

Exhibits are laid out in a sequence of themed displays accessed by ramp and lift, starting at ground level with marine harbour life and a beach display. On the first floor are the shoreline display, virtual reality room, ray tank and sea lab. Freshwater displays are on the second floor. An open balcony provides a breathing space before the riverside exhibits and returns people to daylight.

The level change between the main square and the canal side offers the opportunity to enter the aquarium at both levels, maximising public access to facilities and helping to animate the surroundings, for example with the cafe spilling out onto the canal side. Facilities which are publicly accessible without payment include the foyer, temporary exhibition area, cafe, shop and wc's, all of which have level access.

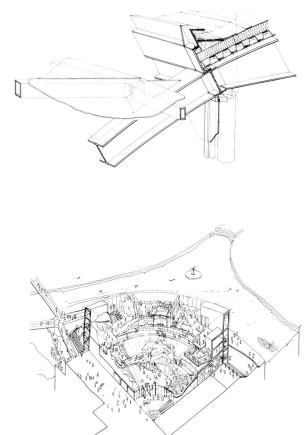

1. BIRMINGHAM FOR PEOPLE

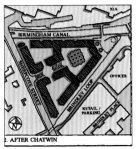

2. AFTER CHATWIN

3. L+S+H DESIGN DEVELOPMENT

4. L+S+H AS BUILT

Lyons Sleeman Hoare

The Triangle

Occupying the triangle site across the Brindley Loop Canal, Symphony Court comprises 143 dwellings, with one-, two-and three-bedroom flats, town houses, maisonettes and penthouses, all with car parking. Developed by Crosby Homes (Midlands), the scheme was largely designed by Lyons Sleeman Hoare, who secured the planning consent, although elevational changes were made thereafter by the developer's architects.

The aim was to create an identifiable place for a residential community within the urban grain of this part of Birmingham, *writes Lyons Sleeman Hoare*. The juxtaposition of the built form to the canal and road systems led to the creation of an internal courtyard and a boulevard parallel to the former line of Nile Street. The new buildings along Sheepcote Street reinforce the streetscape, while town houses placed along the southern boundary to the Brindley Loop Canal have private terraces to the water's edge, providing the opportunity for moorings.

Public and semi-public amenity space is provided across the site. The north-west and east corners of the site form pockets of public space along the canal towpath. A new pedestrian ramp linking Sheepcote Street to this towpath extends the city centre towpath network and provides space both for seating and for public art. Similarly the pocket of public space to the east of the site creates a link between the existing towpath system along the Birmingham Canal and a new public route over the footbridge to the main Brindleyplace development.

The residential accommodation is generally three storeys or more, above a single-storey plinth containing parking. This provides for covered parking within the blocks of flats, thereby allowing the external courtyards to be landscaped.

The former contamination of the land has dictated a hard landscape solution, utilising different materials, colours, texture and patterns. A number of trees and pockets of soft landscaping at key points soften and enhance the built form. In keeping with city guidelines, through-routes are discouraged and so open areas are largely overlooked by adjacent dwellings.

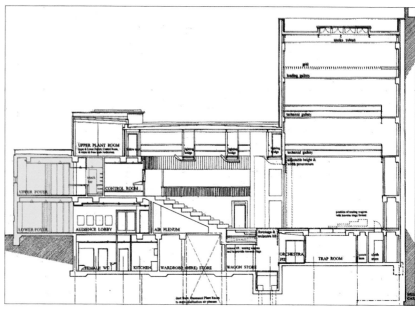

John Chatwin

Crescent Theatre

When Argent acquired Brindleyplace, the Crescent Theatre stood in the centre of the site. Both the 1991 masterplan and the subsequent revision for Argent provided for the theatre, designed by Graham Winteringham, to remain, *writes John Chatwin*. But the backstage space meant that usage of the theatre would always be limited and it was agreed that Argent would build a replacement on the corner of Sheepcote Street and the canal.

The new building would replicate the old theatre's flexible performance spaces but also include additional ancillary spaces to increase use of the theatre. Argent appointed

John Chatwin as architect and theatre consultant Martin Carr to design the technical installation and act for the theatre regarding their operational requirements. After the design of the theatre had been fully established a design & build contract was negotiated with Norwest Holst, who appointed executive architects and engineers for detail design of the shell. Stage and auditorium and acoustic performance remained the responsibility of the original concept team. National Lottery funding was secured from the Arts Council for a separate fit-out contract comprising a studio theatre, enhanced access facilities and public spaces and additional

technical installation in the main auditorium. This was carried out by the Crescent Theatre after completion of the Argent contract.

Foyer spaces and the main auditorium occupy the central volume between the two main stair towers; ancillary spaces are planned on either side. The studio theatre, bar and other social spaces overlook the canal; because the canal is lower than the road, three storeys can be accommodated here, maximising the use of this attractive outlook. On the other side is the double-height workshop and scenery facility, sharing a service yard with the adjacent hotel. The space beneath the auditorium rake is

used to supply air to grilles beneath each seat; air is drawn from the north side of the building, where it is naturally cooled by the canal. The adaptable orchestra pit platform, a second lift and seating wagons moved on air-hover palettes provide for a variety of formats. The Lottery decision was reached just in time to allow us to incorporate in the building contract the additional backstage and enlarged audience lifts. But it was not possible to adapt the entrance and foyer spaces and, as built, the public circulation contains some compromises. But structural provision is in place for the extended foyer to be added at a later date.

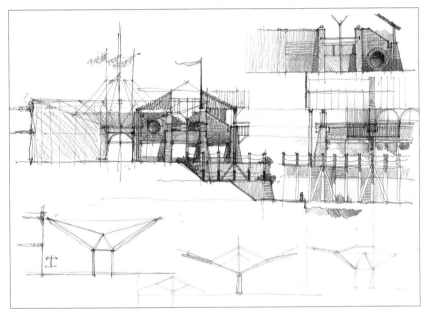

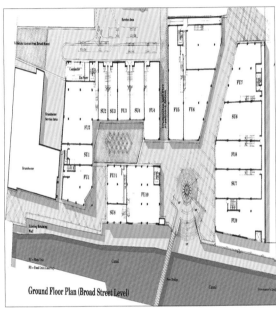

Ground Floor Plan (Broad Street Level)

Benoy

Water's Edge and Car Park

The opening of the Water's Edge in 1995 marked the completion of the first phase of the Brindleyplace development. Located alongside the Birmingham Canal directly opposite the International Convention Centre, it comprises restaurants, bars and shops arranged around a piazza and pedestrian route leading to the main square.

The Water's Edge take its inspiration from Birmingham's 200 year old canal system, *writes Benoy Architects & Designers*. The form of the scheme underwent a long gestation. Close collaboration was required with John Chatwin to ensure that the Water's Edge integrated successfully into the masterplanning framework. The plan is generated both from analysis of pedestrian flows in and around Brindleyplace and from the vistas from Broad Street, the ICC and along the canal. The scheme sits tight to the canal towpath on the edge of the deep sandstone cuffing, directly opposite the ICC piazza and astride the axial line that extends from the ICC mall via a new suspension bridge to the main square.

The pedestrian bridge terminates at the edge of a sheltered piazza some way above water level, around which the components of the Water's Edge are clustered. It is intended that the piazza, which also collects other pedestrian routes permeating the scheme, should be a highly visible centre of concentrated activity, with wide appeal.

The buildings draw on canalside architecture not only in terms of materials, colour and textures but also in the way in which these functional structures jostle against basin, wharf or lock. The resulting composition suggests a permanence and landmark quality not unlike the former brassworks buildings on the site.

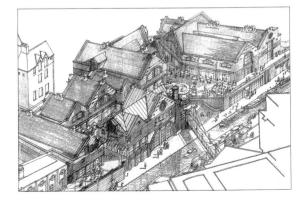

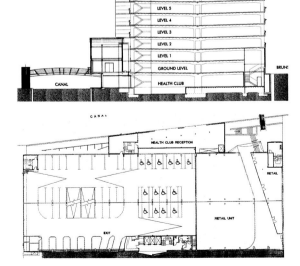

While the office buildings at Brindleyplace include basement parking, the masterplan always posited a separate multi-deck facility to provide the balance of the parking requirement – about 1,000 spaces. A glance at the site plan immediately suggests the simplest and most efficient disposition of the parking bays, *writes Benoy Architects & Designers*. The integration of shopping, cafe and health club facilities, however, provides the opportunity to enliven the £7.9m project and make it more than a simple car parking exercise.

The site abuts the theatre and the Number Four building and has only two main facades, one onto the narrow Brunswick Street and the other addressing the canal. A pedestrian route crosses the site, leading from the main square to a new footbridge spanning the canal, which formed part of the project.

The car park contains nine parking levels with 903 spaces, accessed from Brunswick Street by means of a three-lane entrance and exit system. The in-situ concrete clear-span portals (Hill Cannon Tricon 4) allow for uninterrupted parking, with no columns. Wide ramped slabs (Hill Cannon vertical circulation module) allow rapid but comfortable climb and descent. The car park is planned on a modular basis to allow for areas to be easily segregated for contract parking. Lighting and finish are selected with customer security in mind.

A circulation tower contains lifts and stairs, toilets, information and pay stations. Clad externally with glass blocks set in a steel frame, the tower acts as a landmark to the building when viewed from the square and when illuminated at night shines as a beacon. Floor levels are colour-coded. Both floors and walls are tiled and lifts are glass-fronted for security as well as aesthetic reasons. Externally the modular frame is clad with precoloured panels which cloak the integral reinforced concrete crash barriers.

Anthony Peake Associates

Number One

Number One was the first completed office building in the Brindleyplace development. Argent took the bold decision to go ahead with the speculative £7m project in the recession-ridden days of 1994. The site, designated in the Terry Farrell Partnership masterplan inherited from Rosehaugh, was a 43 x 41 metre 'square' on the corner of Broad Street and Oozells Street that leads directly into the Brindleyplace development. The building completely fills the site footprint, with five floors of 16 metre deep floor plates around a 9 x 11.5 metre atrium, with a 64-car basement below. It provides **68,500** square feet (6,370

square metres) of office space at a construction cost of £87.50 per square foot (£813 per square metre).

In order to add to a corner that counts, *writes Anthony Peake Associates*, our building had to address the lesser scale of its immediate neighbour, a listed church and tower, and to stand as a pointer to the new business district. A corner 'turret' to the side street surmounts a three-storey component, articulated from the main body of the building with an arcade at ground level, celebrating the comer and leading to Brindleyplace.

The main plane of the Broad Street elevation aligns with the adjacent Brasshouse

pub on the city centre grid, thereby forming a diagonal wall against which we set the three-storey 'church-related' element of the composition, orthogonal to Broad Street. The double-height main entrance on Broad Street ends the arcade and skewers the primary compositional planes.

While the building can be seen in the nineteenth-century Birmingham tradition of red-brick monoliths, the detailing reveals the external envelope as a slim, non-loadbearing skin. Reconstituted stone banding articulates special parts and sheds rainwater from the face of brickwork.

The external cladding is heavily insulated and thermally

separated from the in situ concrete frame. The grid of the frame is partly determined by car parking layouts in order to avoid expensive transfer structure. A building management system and fully integrated light-sensing luminaire control system is installed. A 'Very Good' BREEAM (Building Research Establishment Environmental Assessment Method) rating was achieved. Natural lighting is excellent, with the central atrium finished in highly light-reflective materials and abundant perimeter fenestration.

Until the letting agents insisted on provision for multi-tenancy use, involving acoustic and smoke separation, our

When it was completed in 1995, Number One was the first office building at Brindleyplace. Prominently located on Broad Street at the corner with Oozells Street, it represented a 'shop window' for the development taking place behind.

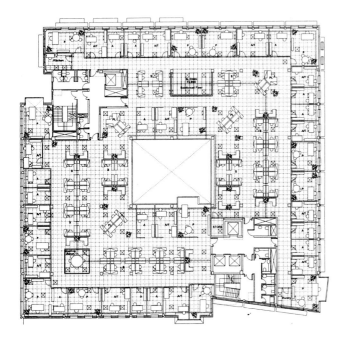

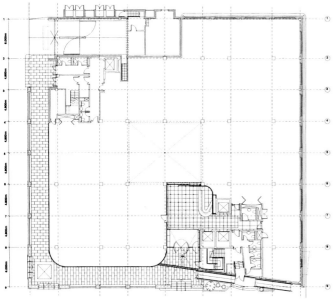

intention had been that the atrium should be open and provide natural ventilation by stack effect. In future, and as and when the traffic on Broad Street diminishes, it would be simple for a single tenant to operate the building without the air conditioning provided.

The service cores were designed for maximum convenience and to ensure an 84% net-to-gross efficiency. Future flexibility is ensured by non-gender specific wc's, naturally lit and ventilated staircases and generously sized lift/vertical service ducts to a high specification.

The floorplates can be space-planned for open or closed office layouts, with raised floors and easily re-positioned luminaire and air supply registers. Special spaces for meeting rooms and terraces have been created where the floor plates are elaborated as a result of external geometries.

From the outset, it was known that construction procurement would be by design & build. Argent knew exactly what they wanted in terms of building standards and insisted that the employer's requirement packages be very tightly drawn. Prior to tender the client consultant team was commissioned to complete detail design (RIBA stage E), with a full watching brief to the end of construction.

Wimpey Construction (now

Number One was conceived as a naturally ventilated office building, with an open-sided atrium providing ventilation by stack effect. In the event, to provide for multi-tenant letting the atrium was closed in and therefore air conditioning was required but it would be possible for a future single occupier to revert to natural ventilation.

Tarmac) won the two-stage design & build tender and their construction professionals rapidly integrated with the client consultant team. Led by the client project manager, the whole team worked harmoniously to finish the building on time, to a very high quality of finish and within budget – showing that if the project is set up properly, design & build can work extremely well.

INTERNAL FINISHES AND DECORATIONS

Office Areas

Walls	Two coat plastered finish to receive 1 mist and three full coats of emulsion paint finish.
Ceilings	600 x 600 x 17 demountable suspended ceiling tiles as Armstrong Microlook Radius GL oe&a supported in exposed white finish 'T' grid oe&a.
Floors	Raised access floors (carpeted by tenant) and finished with hardwood skirtings.
Joinery	Hardwood as specified.
Windows	Aluminium, silver metallic colour coated as outside, with lockable handles. Internal window boards shall be hardwood to match other joinery.

PROJECT
ONE BRINDLEYPLACE

ANTHONY PEAKE ASSOCIATES
CHARTERED ARCHITECTS

TITLE
DETAIL ELEVATION & SECTION SHEET

PRESCOTT STUDIOS

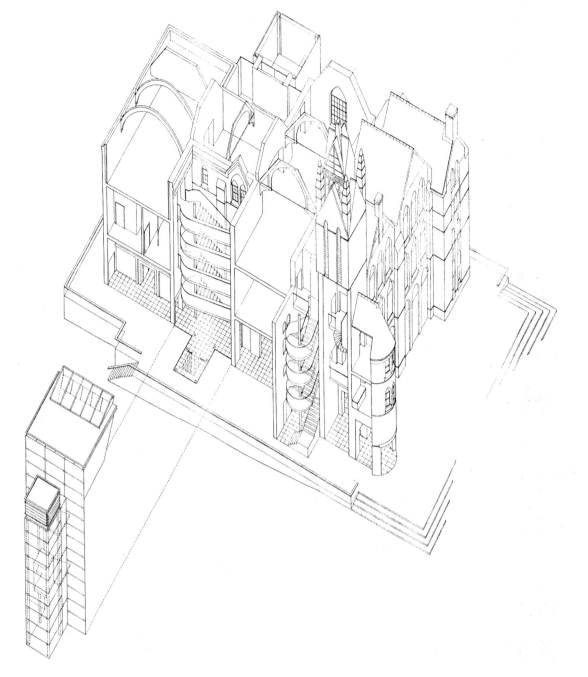

Levitt Bernstein

Ikon Gallery

The conversion of the former Oozells Street School into the new home of the Ikon Gallery is an intrinsic part of the Brindleyplace masterplan. Located between Number One and Number Two, the Ikon Gallery opened to the public in the spring of 1998. The gallery is devoted to temporary exhibitions of the work of living artists.

In 1991 the Ikon Gallery started looking for a new home because the lease on their existing premises was coming to an end, *writes Levitt Bernstein Associates*. Of all the options considered – and despite its ruinous state – Oozells Street School had the greatest potential. It was built in 1877 to the design of Martin & Chamberlain, Birmingham's premier Victorian architects, who built over 40 schools. The original school, designed in a robust and decorative Ruskinian Gothic style, was extended by the same architects in the 1890s and further extensions were built around 1910. The tower, a feature of Martin & Chamberlain schools that formed part of the natural ventilation system, had been removed in the 60s.

The three-storey building is H-shaped in plan. The large linked classrooms on the first and second floors have been converted 4 4,800 square feet (450 square metres) of

Ground, first and second floor plans.
1 Entrance, 2 tower, 3 reception, 4 cafe, 5 shop, 6 lift and stairs, 7 disabled wc, 8 baby change, 9 wcs, 10 workshop office, 11 workshop, 12 service lift, 13 kitchen, 14-17 not shown, 18 education, 19 galleries, 20 meetings, 21 library mezzanine, 22 staff rest room, 23 offices, 24 discovery.
The basement level contains storage, plant, archive and audio visual facilities.

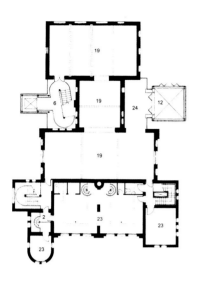

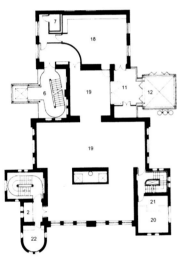

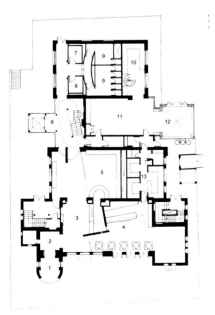

gallery space. The ground floor contains the entrance, shop, cafe and support spaces both for the public and the works of art. A new basement provides further storage, workshop and plant areas.

The school building had no main entrance, simply doors onto two stairs – one for boys and the other for girls and infants. These two stairs have become escape routes, with a new entrance created in the front elevation. To keep the uninterrupted sequence of exhibition spaces, new stairs and lifts have been added outside the original building in a simple manner that contrasts with the highly detailed brick: the route to the galleries, via a glass stair in a glazed enclosure, is intended to be an exhilarating process.

At a late stage in the renovation project, receipt of a European grant allowed the tower to be rebuilt so that, as originally, it forms part of the ventilation design. Internally its full height can be enjoyed on all three levels. The surrounding developments have altered adjoining ground levels and a virtue has been made of this fact by setting the building on a dark slate plinth. This proposal was one of the results of the collaboration with the artist Tania Kovats, following receipt of an Art for Architecture award from the Royal Society of Arts.

The route to the galleries on the first and second floors is via an elegant glass tower standing outside the brick skin of the Victorian school which allows the visitor to feel both outside and inside at the same time,

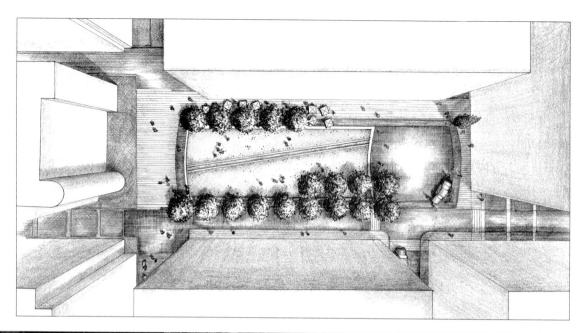

Townshend Landscape

Oozells Square

Oozells Square was not identified as an open space in the original masterplan. But a review of the plan by the team, along with a perceived demand for more restaurant and leisure activities grouped around further open space, led to its designation, *writes Robert Townshend*.

The brief was similar to that for the main square – except that this was to be a square with a strong individual identity, which would complement and not compete with the main square. This was helped by the presence of the former school, which had become the Ikon Gallery, at the east end of the space and by the strongly linear form of the space itself.

We felt that a simple but strong response was required which would connect the two ends of the space, particularly as the buildings to the west had not yet been designed.

To achieve this a rill of water runs diagonally across the space, focusing on the tower of the Ikon Gallery at one end and on a tree at the other. The tree was positioned to frame the views from Broad Street to the entrance to the proposed Number Seven building. The centre of the square, across which the rill runs before disappearing at either end, was depressed to distinguish it from the surrounding circulation routes, as well as to provide a frame into

which sculptor Paul de Monchaux could insert the family of sculptures which he was creating for the space. The area is finished in a self-sealing Raisby gravel, giving it a soft finish when kept raked but allowing it to double as a boules allée during the summer months.

The frame, a limestone step, is reinforced by lines of trees. White flowering cherries were chosen for the brilliance of their colour as well as for the carpet of petals they create, giving a simple but strong event in the calendar. At night the trees are uplit. This is the only light source in the space other than the rill, which is lit from hidden sources beneath

the water at each end. The rill is carved out of blocks of black granite and brings a line of light down to the ground plane. This constantly flowing stream is randomly disturbed by a pulse, creating the illusion of water running uphill.

The pedestrian areas on the upper level are laid in York stone, using pieces of the same dimensions as in the starburst pattern of the main square but in a simple broken bond. Vehicular areas are finished with reclaimed York stone setts retrieved from the remnants of a number of the old roads on the site.

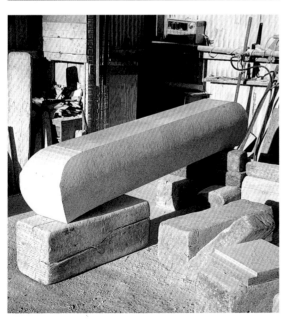

Robert Townshend's landscape design for Oozells Square was well advanced when, in October 1997, I was invited to propose ideas for sculpture, *writes Paul de Monchaux.* Townsend's plan continued some of the themes of the nearby main square, where the symmetry of the space is broken or 'carved' by strong diagonal and curvilinear relief.

Usually, the more 'sculptural' an architectural space is, the more difficult it is to site sculpture in or near it. I discussed this issue with Robert Townsend, who was able to modify the plan of the stone frame of the gravel sculpture area to make a more neutral container for the work. The diagonal relief of the water channel bisecting the stepped stone frame remained to be negotiated as the first term of the composition.

Working with a 1:10 model of the space, I arrived at a scheme where seven granite sculptures formed an inner rectangle that spanned the channel at the point where its diagonal axis meets the centre of the square. The effect of this layout was to provide a three-dimensional counterweight or foil to the drama of the channel diagonal.

The sculptures were made at the De Lank granite quarry in Cornwall, working from scaled and full-sized drawings, 1:10 plaster maquettes and a full-sized plaster model of the curved bench ends. The work was installed in October 1998.

The full-scale realisation of a sculpture often reveals unexpected visual events. One was the focused view of the sculptures from the first landing of the Ikon Gallery staircase. Another was the way the low winter light on the water channel bounced the bridge sculpture's own reflection back on itself – a sundial of light rather than shadow.

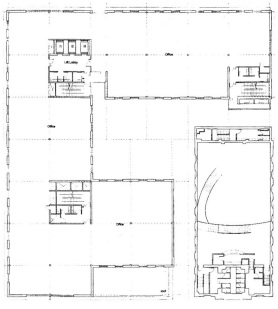

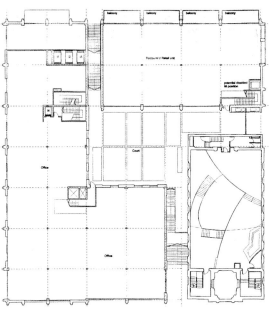

Associated Architects

Number Nine

Number Nine is conceived as a mixed-use building bridging the space between Broad Street and Oozells Square and announcing Brindleyplace to Broad Street. It is adjacent to the grade 2 listed Presbyterian church, dating from 1849, which is prominent in long views in and out of the city.

Number Nine combines 26,800 square feet (2,500 square metres) of restaurant space with 43,000 square feet (4,000 square metres) of offices and 60 parking spaces, *writes Associated Architects*. Maximum flexibility for subdivision was a key consideration, providing small units for both offices and restaurants. The restaurant space and associat-ed service areas occupy the entire site area at ground-floor level and two storeys on Oozells Square. Above this the plan resolves into a 15 metre wide footprint related to the site perimeter, with a first-floor courtyard providing dual aspect for accommodation above. To improve permeabili-ty, a route is developed through the site, creating a space between the building and the church and separating the office entrance from the remainder of the Oozells Square frontage (an influence here was Aalto's Säynätsalo town hall, where the plan allows the component parts to read as individual elements). Where the short axes of

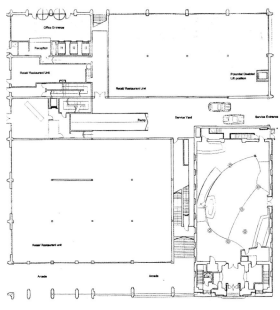

Standing on Broad Street next to the 1849 Presbyterian church, Number Nine complements the first completed Brindleyplace office, Number One, on the other side of the church. The entire ensemble announces the development to the main thoroughfare of Broad Street.

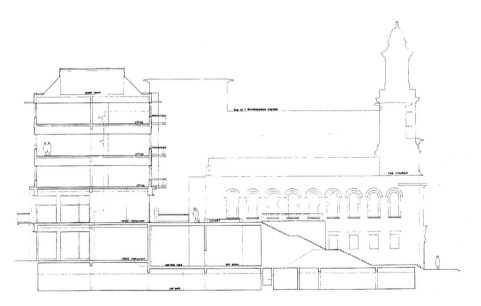

component blocks meet the corners, they are expressed as 'bookends', allowing discreet entrances to be formed relating to the Brindleyplace masterplan. The massing was determined in relationship to the landmark of the church. The building steps down from five storeys in Oozells Square to three in Broad Street, with a two-storey arcade relating to the church parapet. The constant height in Oozells Square forms a common backdrop to the composition.

The Brindleyplace language of buildings with a base, middle and top is employed where it contributes to the street and has a resonance with its neighbours, whether existing or projected. The arcade extends the line of the church parapet; two further storeys are formed in buff brick with punched window openings and the whole surmounted with a lightweight clerestory. Number Nine is overlooked by a number of higher buildings and so the plantroom space is controlled behind a uniform pitched metal roof. Details in the wall planes reflect the structural grid, appearing as control lines and changes in the plane and mass of the masonry elements. Secondary metalwork continues this theme, for example in the arcade as it approaches the church and in a brise-soleil at clerestory level.

Sidell Gibson

Numbers Eight and Ten

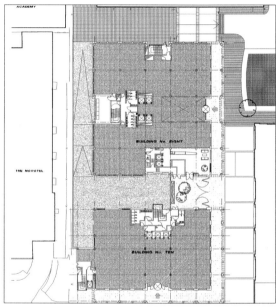

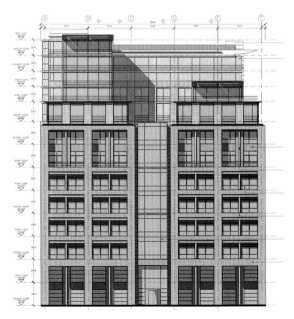

Numbers Eight and Ten occupy the southern-most corner of the site. When they are complete, the two buildings, providing office and residential accommodation, will represent the final chapters in the Brindleyplace story.

Number Eight is a mixed-use development comprising eight floors of office space with five floors of residential accommodation above, *writes Sidell Gibson Partnership.* Positioned at the south-western edge of Oozells Square, it will provide 90,000 square feet (8,370 square metres) of air-conditioned offices with plant provision on every floor , providing optimum flexibility in servicing. The U-shaped floor plates are focused around a central light well, which has full-height, north-facing glazing giving dynamic views across Oozells Square to the surrounding buildings.

Entrance to the offices is via the ground-floor arcade, with the main axis of approach aligning with the facades of the buildings on the south-east edge of the square. From the arcade the brick framework of the facade rises vertically to the seventh-floor cornice, matching the height of the adjoining buildings. Above this level, the first floor of residential accommodation is set back, minimising the impact of the additional storeys. Beyond the eighth

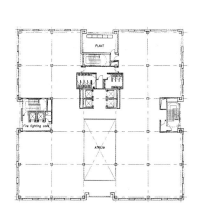

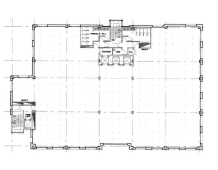

floor, the building steps back again, concealing the upper levels from the ground.

The residential component consists of 38 flats, all with views over Birmingham to the surrounding countryside. Penthouse flats are roofed with over-hanging louvred 'wings'; these act as solar shading to the highly glazed facades below and create a striking silhouette.

Number Ten occupies the southern corner of the Brindleyplace site, with a strong presence on Broad Street. It will provide a high-quality office of 60,000 square feet (5,580 square metres) net over seven floors.

The massing resolves the contrasting scales of Broad Street and Brindleyplace and forms a transitional element between them. In cross section, Number Ten responds to the general scale of Broad Street with a five-storey frontage. Beyond this the facade steps back, forming a terrace at fifth-floor level, before rising a further three storeys (including plant screen) to give a scale relating to the buildings behind. At sixth-floor level, a two-storey bay serves as an intermediate element, in both elevation and section, between the five- and eight-storey components.

The formal symmetry and horizontality of the front elevation is broken by the vertical counterpoint of the glazed stair tower. When viewed looking down Broad Street from the north, this acts as a visual full-stop, marking the edge of the development.

Number Ten is a framed building and this is expressed in its plain brickwork cladding. The red brick framework with its recessed windows evokes nineteenth-century industrial architecture – an effect reinforced by the circular metal columns and recessed double-brick soldier course 'lintels' to the windows. The glazed central bay to the Broad Street elevation expresses the structure behind – ie 15 metre spans of on either side of 7.5 metre core/circulation zone.

The upper-level apartments of Number Eight rise up above the adjacent Number Ten, enjoying spectacular views to the south-east over Birmingham. With five floors of apartments above eight floors of offices, Argent here achieves a longstanding ambition to mix commercial and residential uses within a single building.

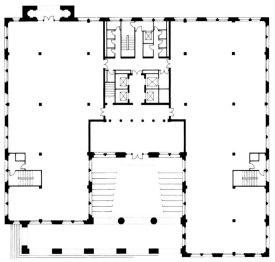

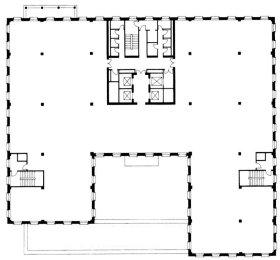

Porphyrios
Associates

Number Seven

Number Seven stands at the gateway to Brindleyplace from Sheepcote Street, addressing both the main square and Oozells Square. The seven-storey building provides 85,000 square feet (7,900 square metres) of office space around an entrance courtyard with basement parking.

The building both forms and is formed by the two adjacent squares, *writes Porphyrios Associates*. Its location suggested a composite building that is both figure and ground, displaying continuity with the urban fabric yet having a distinct figural presence. Its massing is subtractive: an incom-

plete courtyard building that inflects towards the main square. A few steps describe a podium that reconstructs the archaeology of the building's plan. On the side of Oozells Square, a projecting volume steps onto the pavement, announcing the building while also holding the corner.

Allies & Morrison

Number Six

Located between and facing onto both the main square and Oozells Square, Number Six provides 92,000 square feet (8,500 square metres) of office space on seven floors and 4,500 square feet (420 square metres) of restaurant space at ground level facing onto Oozells Square, plus basement parking.

Number Six is the only structure unaffected by the asymmetric disciplines of the masterplan, *writes Allies & Morrison*. Its location at the centre of Brindleyplace is acknowledged in the composition. The tripartite facades to the two squares are calm and open while the side elevations facing the streets are more closed and subordinate.

The entrance route leads from the main square via the colonnade and reception hall to the raised first-floor atrium – a progression reflected in the tripartite division of the elevation. The glazed rooflight set within the inner terrace of the loggia floor illuminates the atrium below. The openings on three sides of the atrium appear as balconies in the five-storey inner volume. The fourth side is formed by the core, where four lifts open to landings at ground- and first-floor levels and via timber bridges to the atrium above. Simple, repeated, gun-metal coloured windows occupy each of the deeply-recessed openings in the warm red brick facade.

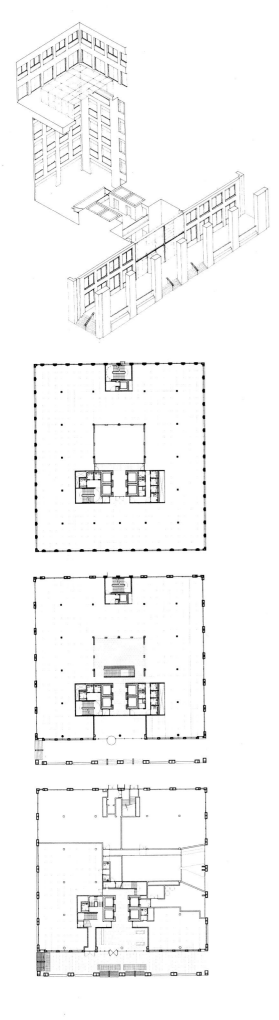

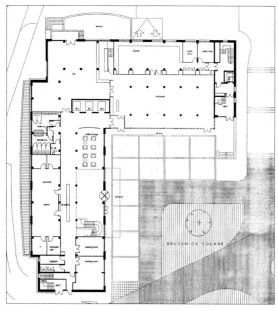

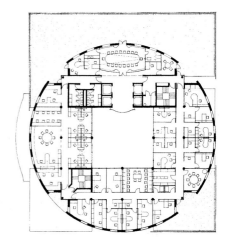

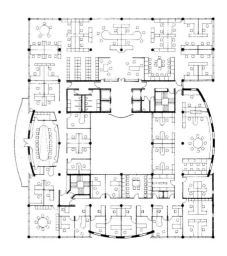

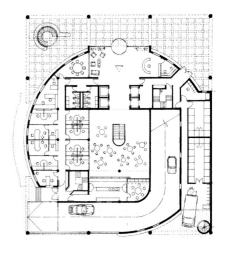

Hulme
Upright
Weedon

Hotel

City Inn is an eight-storey building sitting beside the main vehicular entrance to Brindleyplace from Sheepcote Street. This is the third in a series of new hotels being built by First Stop Hotels, *writes Hulme Upright Weedon*. The deep, curved cornice and vertical strip windows are elements common to all City Inns, whereas the facades – terracotta-coloured brick panels framed by a recessed channel – are unique to the one at Brindleyplace. The square shape of the site combined with the 14 metre optimum width for each wing of the hotel created the opportunity to increase the size of Brunswick Square by setting the main frontage of the building back from Number Five and embracing a larger open space with an L-shaped structure. This has created more space for the vehicular comings and goings at the hotel entrance and also allowed for the creation of restaurant terraces, thereby bringing activity to the new square during warmer months. Similarly, on the west side of the building, the hotel bar spills out onto terraces which address the space in front of the new Crescent Theatre.

Edward Cullinan Architects

Number Two (project)

Edward Cullinan Architects produced two designs for Number Two, both of which emphasised the pivotal position of the building in the masterplan.

The first created a drum emerging from a cube which had a front bay forming a portico to the square, *writes Edward Cullinan Architects*. There was a deliberate contrast between the treatment of the drum, in cobalt blue render, and the fully glazed curtain walling to the square. The building was to be naturally ventilated, with the lantern over the central atrium acting as a thermal chimney.

The second scheme created a pivotal drum at the corner of the building, which would be visible as one approached from the canal and city centre. Compositionally the building again had two contrasting elements – smooth render with big punched-hole windows for the cube and curtain walling for the drum.

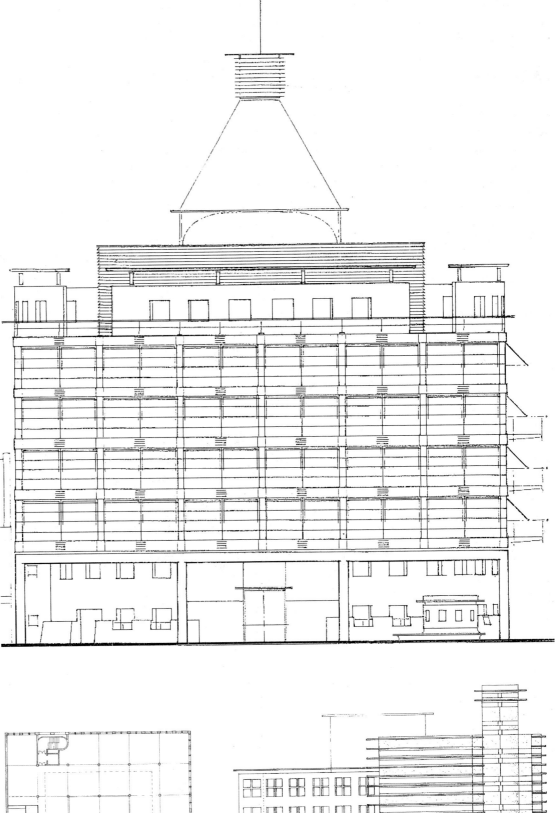

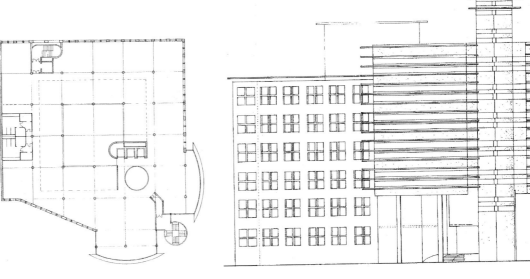

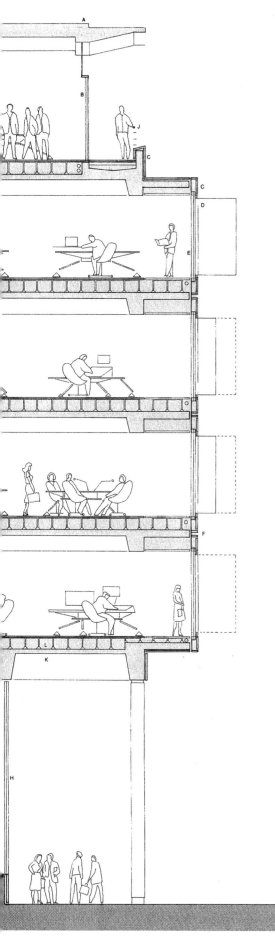

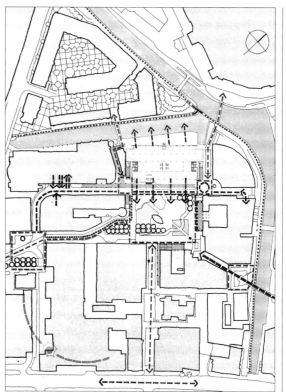

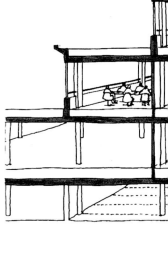

Lifschutz Davidson

Number Four (project)

Lifschutz Davidson's proposal for Number Four incorporated a series of screens to protect the south-facing main elevation. As the sun moves across the facade the punched-louvre stainless steel screens gradually pivot to reduce solar gain. The entrance, marked by a canopy, is aligned on Oozells Street.

Anthony Peake Associates

Number Four (project)

At the end of 1993 Argent entered a competition to provide Mercury Communications with a purpose-built 180,000 square foot (16,740 square metre) headquarters. The distinguished building services consultant Andrew Wilkes had been appointed head of Mercury's premises department

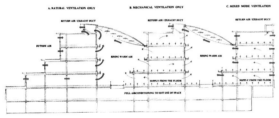

and wanted a building that met his concerns about the workplace environment.

It seemed to be the chance that we and Argent had been waiting for, *writes Anthony Peake Associates*: a sophisticated major player who would allow us to break new ground with a purpose-built headquarters, removing the usual need for an office building to fit safely into the usual 'developer essentials'. Taking the site for Number Four, we developed an E-shaped plan with the fingers pointed north over the Brindley Loop Canal. The spine of the E comprised a seven-storey frontage to the main square with two huge glazed atria between the fin-gers connecting the various parts and opening the whole building up to the north. Stack effect ventilation within the atria drew fresh air in via a tall glazed wall from across the canal while a simple, low-pressure floor plenum with local floor fans permitting individual control of worplaces. In many ways it would have been a remarkable and ground-breaking project.

After a year or so however Mercury went cold on the whole idea and in the end the scheme came to nothing. We were then asked by Argent to develop an (inevitably much less daring) scheme for a speculative office for the site (right) but this too remained unbuilt.

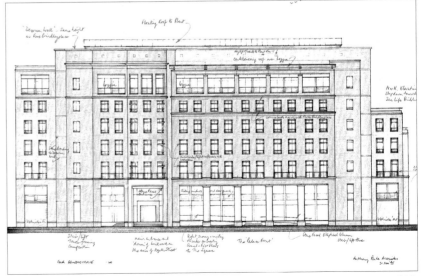

Chapter six: A model for urban regeneration

Patsy Healey

It is often said that the way to revitalise our cities and make them more sustainable is by mixed-use development projects on brownfield sites in existing urban landscapes. If this is to happen, development companies will be needed to provide the expertise to release such sites into a position in the property market where commercial viability can be sustained. While much attention focuses on flagship schemes in London, these are often atypical and not necessarily therefore a reliable guide to what is needed across UK cities as a whole. In this context, the story of Birmingham's Brindleyplace offers valuable lessons on what it takes to create a new piece of city, which adds a new location to the mix of places which compose the city.

Visitors to Birmingham with long memories will remember a city centre stifled by its ring road, with a drab and under-developed retail and commercial core. Those who have not visited the city centre lately are in for a big surprise. While other cities have been feeling the pressure of competition from out-of-town locations, Birmingham in the past decade has produced a new and distinctive city centre. On foot you can walk from New Street station through a series of new or newly configured and impressive public squares and arcades, including Victoria Square, Chamberlain Square and Centenary Square. This enjoyable experience is the result of sustained and consistent action by the city council. Streets have been pedestrianised, roadways have been pushed underground, traffic flows have been re-organised, a huge investment has been made in leisure and cultural facilities (including the International Convention Centre and the National Indoor Arena) and a great deal of creative attention has been given to the design of the public realm in terms of paving, levels, sculpture, flows and signage.

From Centenary Square and the International Convention Centre, you can now walk on to the refurbished canalside and over a bridge into Brindleyplace. In doing so, you traverse a vast area of former metal-bashing industry, assembled through voluntary and compulsory purchase over the years by the city council and converted through imaginative investments into a new focus for the city's cultural activities. Without Birmingham city council's energy and strategic imagination, there would be no Brindleyplace as it is today.

This strategic orientation was no easy achievement. Despite a municipal tradition of proactive development, the city council in the 80s and 90s was squeezed of resources and increasingly forced to turn to diverse sources to fund its plans. And although there was a consensus among many councillors, officers and business interests about the importance of the city centre to Birmingham's economy, there was also criticism of the council's approach on social and environmental grounds. As a result 'strategy' came to be understood in a special way. Rather than a comprehensive plan in the style of the 50s, the city worked with a clear but flexible idea: the creation of a city centre to be proud of, re-using former industrial sites as necessary to achieve this. This goal focused the attention of funders, investors and implementers. In realisation, however, it was continually changing in specifics as new opportunities and challenges came along.

Brindleyplace has benefited from this 'flexi-strategy'. It is located some distance from the traditional city centre core, to the west of the canal basin which provided the rationale for its original development over two centuries ago. The site was contaminated, in multiple ownership and surrounded by areas of mixed low-cost housing, industry, offices and shops.

In such a location, attracting development interest requires a complete transformation of image. At Brindleyplace this was achieved by long-term commitment, steadily piecing together opportunities as they came along, within the context of a flexible design brief. In effect, it is a new urban neighbourhood with a mixture of leisure, retail, cultural, office and housing uses which has also generated spin-off effects around it, especially along Broad Street and the canalside.

As well as the strategic commitment of the city council, a number of factors were crucial. One was simply scale. It would have been very difficult to achieve such a transformation by piecemeal redevelopment and a key investment decision early on was to landscape the site, giving investors confidence in the future of the development. Another was the masterplan, initially produced by Terry Farrell (with inputs on pedestrian flows from Bill Hillier of the Bartlett School) and subsequently revised by ex-Farrell partner John Chatwin in collaboration with developer Argent. The masterplan focused on a few key features, notably the squares and canal frontage, and the axis from Centenary Square through to the heart of the site. Otherwise, the site was divided into developable plots. A few general conditions apply to each plot, to produce some commonality of massing and frontage. Otherwise, the building form is left to a mixture of commercial considerations and designer imagination.

Crucial also was the sum paid for the site by the eventual developers. Thanks to the collapse of the 80s property boom, which brought into receivership the original developer Rosehaugh, the site was secured by Argent for £3m, a fraction of its previous value. The message for city councils should be that development on such sites is no cash cow with which to stock council coffers, at least in the short term. Either the council (or a specialist arms-length agency) has to take on the site and act as master developer or the site should be handed over to a private sector 'master developer' at a low value, with the council retaining a financial interest as partner in the project.

Another key factor in the success of Brindleyplace was the development company. Argent has specialised in a limited portfolio of complex projects on difficult sites; with an astute understanding of the ups and downs of speculative property development markets, it avoided overexposure in the late 80s, preferring to work on a few sites over the long term. The emphasis has been on quality, collaboration, partnership and good site management. The commitment to quality has been important in building and maintaining the reputation of the area as a distinctive new neighbourhood. Collaboration is evident in the emphasis on good working relations with the city council, architects and contractors, with considerable effort going into initial briefing before design work starts. Partnership occurs at many levels, from the overall development company set up for the site, to the mix of experts working on specific projects, and the approach to the management of the site post-development. Site management focuses on maintaining the public realm assets; smoothing the potential tensions in the fine grain of the different uses and ambiences at different times of day; getting all parties to agree about future management arrangements; and establishing links with the disadvantaged neighbourhoods

abutting the site. This takes a great deal of effort, but is crucial to sustaining the confidence of actual and future occupiers and investors.

Working in a context such as this, there are no quick fixes for the development company nor can there be short-term profit-taking. When development is dependent on private sector investment, the task of the 'master-developer' and the city council is to reduce the riskiness inherent in the transformation of brownfield sites into sustainable new pieces of city. Argent shows that the private sector can display this commitment as strongly as any public sector agency.

Faced with the need to attract both investors and occupiers to the area, development management has involved continual re-negotiation of both the overall concept of the area and the design of individual buildings. Although mixed use was inherited from the original brief, the way the mix worked out depended on market conditions. Initially, market conditions were difficult and residential projects were the easiest to realise; but this has meant that the housing area is visibly 'gated off' from the rest of the development (to which indeed residents later objected vociferously). Restaurants and bars on the canal waterfront were immediately successful but then created problems for the security, safety and peacefulness of other parts of the site. Although the site is mixed-use, the plots are in single use and there have been difficulties in generating the volume of trade required for retail. Finally however a mixed-use building is being completed on one of the plots and others are planned – an affirmation that a new kind of niche market has been created.

With skill and commitment over the long-term, Argent and the city council have created a new urban neighbourhood. Brindleyplace is a lively place in the evenings with restaurants, clubs and pubs; an office location to complement the old office core in Colmore Row; a cultural location with an art gallery and theatre; and a city centre residential neighbourhood. But as an example of sustainable urban living for the twenty-first century, it reflects some of the disjointed thinking of the 90s. Although easily accessible on foot from the city centre, the area is not linked to a coherent public transport strategy. As yet, no tram route takes the visitor from the nearest stations to Brindleyplace and so

Brindleyplace from the air, with only the Water's Edge completed and Number One and the main square under construction; and 1994 development model showing Numbers One, Three, Four (the Peake/Mercury design) and Five and the new Crescent Theatre.

many workers and visitors (and probably most residents) are car-dependent. To the west, the entry to the site is via a welcoming roundabout. And here too is another disjunction. Although the frontage to Broad Street merges easily into the street scene, residents of the adjoining neighbourhoods face this new urban fabric from across the roundabout and a dividing road. With its 90s buildings and gateway entry, the development is markedly different from the adjoining areas to which, in its present form, it seems to present its back. Responding to a shift in local politics and the new rhetoric in national politics, Argent is making a praiseworthy attempt to develop relations between the companies occupying the site and residents' groups in the adjoining areas. The canalside walkways provide an attractive public realm resource and a pedestrian and bicycle route to the city centre for Birmingham's inner-city residents. But the site does not flow into the surrounding neighbourhoods in the way that it flows across the canal into the ICC and Centenary Square.

In practice, the city council had a vision for their city centre but this was not linked to a spatial vision for the evolution and interaction of the neighbourhoods across the city. And the new residents of Brindleyplace, nervous about their surroundings, reassure themselves with protective gates and barriers, in addition to the assertive presence of cctv across the site. The way forward for our cities is surely to build positive connections into the fabric of the city, not reinforce barriers. But fostering the inclusive city co-exists uneasily with creating market niches for city centre living and working.

The Brindleyplace project provides some hope that the vision of urban renaissance can be realised if the context and conditions are right. But this is where the problem lies. In British cities in the 90s, there were few places where these conditions prevailed, except where the subsidies and organisational muscle of an Urban Development Corporation were available. In the first decade of the next millennium, many city councils are likely to develop a more strategic orientation to the development and management of their cities. But except in the few cities where there is real pent-up demand for city centre activities, reinforced by co-ordinated planning and transport policies, it will be very difficult to generate sufficient value in the development

process to attract private investment.

The implication, confirmed by experience from Europe and the US, is clear. If brownfield sites are to be transformed into market opportunities, the public sector must be prepared to invest a large amount, over the long-term, and in line with a coherent but flexible vision for the locality. This means shaping market conditions, not just responding to them. And if the commercially viable parts of our cities are to enhance the complex mix of the contemporary city, finding ways of integrating rather than segregating different parts of the city will be at a premium. This suggests that the policy agenda for cities should be less about capturing funding for particular projects, as it has been in the competitive project-based financial environment of the 90s, and more about establishing long-term financing mechanisms, encouraging local authorities and others to develop forward-looking local visions and shaping local property markets.

Brindleyplace in spring 1999, with Oozells Square constructed, the adjacent Number Nine nearing completion and the service core of Number Six already erected on site. The canalside Triangle housing comprises 143 flats, townhouses, maisonettes and penthouses, all with parking.

Credits

Masterplan/infrastructure/main square
Urban design/masterplan: John Chatwin; landscape architect: Townshend Landscape Architects; traffic/infrastructure: Ove Arup & Partners; access consultant: Gavin Tait; lighting: DHE; employer's agent/qs: Silk & Frazier; contractor: Tilbury Douglas; sculptor: Miles Davies.

Water's Edge
Architect: Benoy; structural engineer: Ove Arup & Partners; landscape architect: Townshend Landscape Architects; employer's agent/qs: Silk & Frazier; contractor: Tilbury Douglas; contractor's architect: Temple Cox Nicholls.

Oozells Street School refurbishment
Architect: Levitt Bernstein; employer's agent/qs: Silk & Frazier; structural engineer: Peel & Fowler; contractor: Tilbury Douglas.

Number One
Architect: Anthony Peake Associates; structural/m&e engineer: Ove Arup & Partners; employer's agent/qs: Silk & Frazier; contractor: Wimpey Construction; contractor's architect: Weedon Partnership; contractor's structural engineer: Curtins Consulting Engineers; contractor's m&e engineer: Hoare Lea & Partners.

Number Two
Architect: Allies & Morrison; structural/m&e engineer: Ove Arup & Partners; employer's agent/qs: Silk & Frazier; contractor: Wimpey/Tarmac Construction; contractor's architect: Weedon Partnership; contractor's structural engineer: Curtins Consulting Engineers; contractor's m&e engineer: Hoare Lea & Partners.

Number Three
Architect: Porphyrios Associates; structural/m&e engineer: Ove Arup & Partners; employer's agent/qs: Davis Langdon & Everest; contractor: Kyle Stewart (HBG Construction); detailed design: Kyle Stewart Design Services.

Number Four
Architect: Stanton Williams; structural engineer: Curtins Consulting Engineers; m&e engineer: Hoare Lea & Partners; employer's agent/qs: Silk & Frazier; contractor: Tarmac Construction; contractor's architect: Weedon Partnership.

Number Five
Architect: Sidell Gibson Partnership; structural/m&e engineer: Ove Arup & Partners; employer's agent/qs: Silk & Frazier; contractor: Kyle Stewart; detailed design: Kyle Stewart Design Services.

Number Six
Architect: Allies & Morrison; structural engineer: Curtins Consulting Engineers; m&e engineer: Hoare Lea & Partners; employer's agent/qs: Silk & Frazier; contractor: Tarmac Construction; contractor's architect: Hulme Upright Weedon.

Number Nine
Architect: Associated Architects; structural/m&e engineer: Ove Arup & Partners; employer's agent/qs: Silk & Frazier; contractor: HBG Construction; detailed design: Kyle Stewart Design Services.

Cafe
Architect: CZWG; structural engineer: Kara Taylor; electrical design: NG Bailey; mechanical design: F Bailey; employer's agent/qs: Silk & Frazier; contractor: Kyle Stewart (HBG Construction); detailed design: Kyle Stewart Design Services.

Multi-storey car park
Architect: Benoy; structural engineer: Hill Cannon; m&e engineering: NG Bailey; traffic consultant: Ove Arup & Partners; employer's agent/qs: Silk & Frazier; contractor: Norwest Holst.

Crescent Theatre
Architect: John Chatwin; m&e consultant: NG Bailey; structural engineer: Edward Roscoe; acoustic consultant: Arup Acoustics; theatre consultant: Carr & Angier; contractor: Norwest Holst; contractor's architect: Temple Cox Nicholls.

Oozells Square
Landscape architect: Townshend Landscape Architects; sculptor: Paul de Monchaux; employer's agent/qs: Silk & Frazier; traffic consultant: Ove Arup & Partners; contractor: HBG Construction; detailed design: Kyle Stewart Design Services.

Number Eight
Architect: Sidell Gibson Partnership; structural/m&e engineer: Ove Arup & Partners; employer's agent/qs: Silk & Frazier.

Number Seven
Architect: Porphyrios Associates; structural/m&e engineer: Ove Arup & Partners; employer's agent/qs: Silk & Frazier; contractor: HBG Construction; detailed design: Kyle Stewart Design Services.

Number Ten
Architect: Sidell Gibson Partnership.

Hotel
Architect: Hulme Upright Weedon; structural/m&e engineer: Blyth & Blyth; employer's agent/qs: Gardiner & Theobald; interior design: Thompson & Macleod.

Triangle housing (Symphony Court)
Architect: Lyons Sleeman Hoare; structural engineer: John Newton & Partners; contractor: Kendrick Construction; client: Crosby Homes (Midlands).

National Sealife Centre
Architect: Foster & Partners; structural engineer: Ove Arup & Partners; qs: Geoffrey Nicholls Associates; project manager: Cyril Sweett Project Consultants; contractor: Taylor Woodrow; client: Vardon Attractions.

Institute of Electrical Engineers
Architect: David Robotham; contractor: Kendrick Construction.

Greenalls pub
Architect: John Dixon & Associates; contractor: Curbishley Construction.

Ikon Gallery
Architect: Levitt Bernstein; qs: Silk & Frazier; structural engineer: Peel & Fowler; services engineer: HL Dawson; lighting: John Johnson/Lightwaves; artist: Tania Kovats; contractor: Tarmac Construction.

Photography
Martine Hamilton Knight (front cover), Paul Cordwell, Nick Short, Tony Brien, Russ Capps, Sean Gallagher, Simon Hazelgrove, Jon O'Brien, Alastair Carew-Cox, Christian Powell, Brian Borrett, HBG Construction, Charlotte Wood. Historic views of Birmingham: Norman Bartlam, Housing Education Initiative.

Index